## PRAISE FOR THE BOOK

"There's a certain dynamic to the director-actor relationship that's undefinable. Not many Indian film-makers I know have tried to analyse its intricacies. That's what makes Suman Ghosh's 'memoir' such an important work in the corpus of writing on cinema in India. It's warm, it's intimate and brings to light so many unknown facets to the interactions between Soumitra Chatterjee and the director who gave him some of his most well-regarded films and characters from the last phase of his career. I am glad that Suman has penned this tribute to Soumitra Chatterjee for readers to partake of a special bond." – *Aparna Sen, film-maker and actor*

"The first Bengali film that I saw was *Sonar Kella*, in Kolkata, in 1975. I went home with images not only of the film but also of Feluda, and the actor, whom I discovered over the years and came to admire and love, Soumitra-da Chatterjee. And in recent years, I was able to see another side to Soumitra-da through the films of Suman Ghosh, whom I find most remarkable as a film-maker.

"*Soumitra Chatterjee: A Film-maker Remembers* is an insightful behind-the-scenes study of a legendary actor through the eyes of a brilliant film-maker, Suman Ghosh, revealing the man, the thespian, his processes and world-view. This tribute – a love letter of admiration and gratitude – is a film in itself and in movie parlance, I would say, 'Not to be missed!'" – *Ashutosh Gowariker, film-maker*

"The author with utmost respect gives the reader an opportunity to dive into the inner realms of one of India's greatest actors, Soumitra Chatterjee." – *Adil Hussain, actor*

"Suman Ghosh has touched the soul of a great artist with whom he shared wonderful times. I consider Soumitra a darling of our cultural world. A man for all seasons. A very intimate book on the maestro." – *Goutam Ghose, film-maker*

"I knew Soumitra-da way before he knew me. I grew up watching so many of his films. That was the time I didn't even know I would ever act. So he was my teacher without either of us knowing it!

"And then in 2006, *Podokkhep* fell into my lap. When Suman Ghosh called me up for his first film and dangled the carrot that I would play Soumitra-da's daughter, I jumped at it. Suman, I will always be grateful to you for that. I already knew Soumitra-da was a supremely versatile and authentic performer but when I met him I also got to see an incredibly kind, funny and loving person. And he was that to every single person whose life he touched.

"The news of his passing away was devastating. Both for the world of cinema and theatre but also personally to every single person who had known him. I miss him deeply."

*– Nandita Das, actor and film-maker*

"I was a great fan of Soumitra-da right from the time of *Jhinder Bondi*. He was a great human being and an eternal legend. Writing about him and this book in a few words will be impossible. He will always be an inspiration for actors of all generations. Wherever he is, I am sure he will be blessing us. A great effort by Suman. All the best to him and the book." *– Mithun Chakraborty, actor*

"Suman Ghosh's illuminating memoir about Soumitra Chatterjee, a risk-taking explorer who always had a fascination for life, is a manual for cinephiles. Soumitra-da will always remain my 'APU', the thespian, a polymath with a command over art and science." *– Shoojit Sircar, film-maker*

"A very insightful and heartfelt piece of work from someone who has carefully observed the artiste from close quarters, but with a desired degree of objectivity. Loved it."

*– Parambrata Chattopadhyay, actor and film-maker*

# SOUMITRA CHATTERJEE

## A FILM-MAKER REMEMBERS

First published in 2022 by

**Om Books International**

**Corporate & Editorial Office**
A-12, Sector 64, Noida 201 301
Uttar Pradesh, India
Phone: +91 120 477 4100
Email: editorial@ombooks.com
Website: www.ombooksinternational.com

**Sales Office**
107, Ansari Road, Darya Ganj,
New Delhi 110 002, India
Phone: +91 11 4000 9000
Fax: +91 11 2327 8091
Email: sales@ombooks.com
Website: www.ombooks.com



ISBN: 978-93-92834-17-2

Printed in India

10 9 8 7 6 5 4 3 2 1

# SOUMITRA CHATTERJEE

## A FILM-MAKER REMEMBERS

Suman Ghosh

Om Books International

*For my daughters, Maya and Leela … hope this book provides you a window to your 'Sonar Kella' Dadu*

# Contents

# Acknowledgements

In 2005 when I came to Kolkata to make my debut film, *Podokkhep*, I was taking a plunge from the world of academia to the world of cinema and that too in a different country and milieu from where I lived. Since then I have formed a core team who have not only been co-workers in my journey but have become family. Apart from the wonderful cast and crew in the films in which I have worked, I want to mention my group which has been with me over the last fifteen years. My chief assistant director, Avijit Chaudhuri, my super-efficient production team headed by Saubhik Das and the other team members, Bhola, Subir, Dipankar, Haru, Dadu, Gopal and Birju. My journey with Soumitra-kaku has been intertwined with them. I wish to thank the late Deepa-kakima (Chatterjee) and her children Poulomi-di and Bubu-da for making me part of their family.

I wish to thank Nirmala Chhaochharia without whose support on so many things I could not have continued my journey. Maa and Babuji for their unquestionable faith in me and for being my biggest supporters. To Sarmila-di, for giving me the courage to pursue my dreams when I was planning to dive into the world of films. To Dada and Chhordabhai, for always being there. For Maya, Leela and Vidhi for providing the support and ambience at home.

At a professional level related to this book, I wish to thank the Anandabazar Group for generously allowing me to use two of the pieces which appeared in their publications originally; to *Cinemaazi*, for the essay that forms the prologue to the book; and to Om Books International for the care with which they have published the book. Finally, my editor Shantanu Ray Chaudhuri, for being there throughout the writing process and urging me to probe my relationship with Soumitra-kaku further.

# Foreword

## Sharmila Tagore

Soumitra Chatterjee is a legend. Even after a year of his passing, there has been no let-up of the tributes that continue to pour in. Soumitra Chatterjee had captured the imagination of the people of Bengal and made a place in their hearts. His last journey was a testament to that. All of Kolkata was on the streets bidding him farewell with flowers, music and poetry.

Soumitra Chatterjee belonged to that rare breed of actors who could keep his audience spellbound over five decades. In a world where an actor past his prime often finds himself starved of good material, Soumitra continued to get superlative roles. A young crop of film-makers like Suman Ghosh wrote scripts keeping Soumitra in mind. In his later years, he gave many notable performances. In Suman's own *Podokkhep*, *Peace Haven* and *Basu Poribar*, in Shiboproshad Mukherjee and Nandita Roy's *Belaseshe* and Atanu Ghosh's *Mayurakshi* (both films Suman talks about in the book as being among Soumitra Chatterjee's best), to name a few, he scintillates and sparkles.

Suman Ghosh's memoir on his professional and personal relationship with Soumitra is a welcome addition to the existing literature on Indian cinema. His nuanced and subtle understanding of what makes an actor-director collaboration is very interesting. It is fascinating to read about, for instance, a particularly difficult long scene in *Dwando* and the sheer ease and brilliance with which Soumitra executes it, physicalizing the director's imagination. These are the hidden gems a viewer watching the film on screen can often miss. This book is replete with many anecdotes that make it extremely readable. The way Suman sifts through diverse aspects of Soumitra's characters in the films they worked together provides a remarkable perspective on the craft of performative arts. But Soumitra was more than just a film actor. He was a poet, painter, translator, writer – and in this book we get a close glimpse of these aspects of his life. Imagine translating portions of James Joyce's novella or delving into Jibanananda Das for a film's climax! Simply marvellous.

I have been fortunate enough to work with Soumitra Chatterjee in quite a few films, beginning with *Apur Sansar* – the film with which both of us began our journey in the world of cinema. It is particularly gratifying to see Suman Ghosh mention *Barnali* as amongst the finest of Soumitra's oeuvre. I too have fond memories of us working together and it is also one of my favourite films. I am happy to see Suman quote Pauline Kael in the context of our work together.

I have had the privilege of observing Soumitra, up-close and personal, as an actor and as a human being. We have had many stimulating adda sessions. I can vouch for his remarkable range of interests which enlivened and enlightened these addas. I have always longed to do a recorded conversation with Soumitra. I felt I could have got him to speak in a way that he had not done before – more personal and less academic – which would capture his vitality and genius. I regret that didn't happen.

His was a very strong, clear and well-informed voice and we had much to learn from him. Now that he is no more, a significant portion of Bengal's cinematic and performative history is lost to us forever. I am happy that Suman Ghosh has compiled his memories of working with Soumitra in this book and that it is being published for all of us to enjoy and cherish.

# Author's Note

Bengalis of our generation do not even recollect when we first became conscious about personalities such as Rabindranath Tagore, Satyajit Ray, Uttam Kumar or Soumitra Chatterjee. It is as if they are dinned into us at birth. Soumitra Chatterjee's Feluda was a part of our psyche while growing up.

Much later in life when I started making films I came to know the iconic Soumitra Chatterjee as he was the protagonist of my debut film. I feel extremely fortunate and blessed that he was an integral part of five of my films for the next fifteen years. Over time, the artistic and the personal relationship coalesced and he became my friend, philosopher and guide.

He was by far the most vibrant person I have met. His lust for life knew no bounds. Whether through literature, through poetry, through films, through his interactions with people, through theatre, it was as if he wanted to perpetually soak in the delirium of life and be bathed in all its beauty. His mind was like a blank canvas, ready to be painted with colours. That was true of him as an actor too. Ironically, to render one's mind a blank canvas one has to enrich it to such an extent that it is possible to attain that mystical space.

Hence directors over the last sixty years could paint myriad characters – be it Apu, Mayurbahon, Khit-da, or King Lear – on him. He was ready for more, with younger directors, with newer mediums, newer formats. He was like the protagonist in Scott Fitzgerald's story 'The Curious Case of Benjamin Button' who ages in reverse. Soumitra Chatterjee was the embodiment of Benjamin Button. As the years went by he became more and more like a child. Alas, life had its own story to tell. On 15 November 2020 he left this world and at a personal level left me fatherless.

I still can't forget his smile, his laughter, his jokes, the knowledge he imparted, but mainly his presence. It was as if he would be there, always … like the age-old banyan tree.

Writing this book was a cathartic experience for me. Yes, it was painful to relive the memories. But who said that all pain is bad? Writing this helped me emerge from the deep sorrow that had engulfed me after his demise. This is not an analysis of Soumitra Chatterjee's life and work. So I do not even attempt to be objective in my writing. Can one truly be objective about one's father? Rather, I have tried to share anecdotes about him as a person and as an actor which can only provide a glimpse of the person he was. I sincerely hope that readers will enjoy the book as much as I have enjoyed writing it.

# MEMORY, AGEING AND DEATH

## Suman Ghosh's 'Experiments' with Soumitra Chatterjee[1]

Shantanu Ray Chaudhuri

*'I prayed to rediscover my childhood, and it has come back, and I feel that it is just as difficult as it used to be, and that growing older has served no purpose at all.'* – Rainer Rilke

It says something about the film awards system in our country that Soumitra Chatterjee received his first National Award for Best Actor in 2006! But it also says a lot about the film that fetched him the award and the film-maker who made it. *Podokkhep*, directed by Suman Ghosh. What makes it even more creditable is that this was Ghosh's directorial debut. Over the next decade and a half, Ghosh went on to create an enviable body of work with Soumitra Chatterjee in the lead – in films that comprise the best of the legend's latter-day performances. In fact, over the course of a ten-hour-long interview session that I had with him, the actor singled out Ghosh for special mention among

1 This essay was first published in *Cinemaazi* on 18 January 2021. Thanks to Sumant Batra and *Cinemaazi* for permission to reproduce this in the book.

contemporary directors whose work excited him. No wonder that between 2006 and 2019, he acted in four films helmed by Ghosh: *Podokkhep* (2006), *Dwando* (2009), *Peace Haven* (2015) and *Basu Poribar* (2019). (I leave out 2012's *Nobel Chor*, where the thespian had a guest appearance.)

Looking back, watching the films all over again in the months leading up to the actor's death and after, I was struck by a thematic unity that binds them. This is not to say that the films are similar in any way. In fact, no two films could be more dissimilar than the allegorical piece of black humour that *Peace Haven* is and the almost-gothic chamber drama *Basu Poribar*. Yet, running through all four films like a subterranean thread I discerned the universal themes of memory, ageing and death – the nebulous nature of our memories, the loneliness inherent in growing old and the inevitability of death. I am not sure if the film-maker had any such unity in mind – in casting Soumitra Chatterjee in these characters – or if the films developed organically, and I was reading meanings in them given the backdrop against which I re-watched them. But it does make for an interesting way to look at the four films as a single unit.

In an earlier interaction with me, Suman Ghosh had mentioned, 'As far as hobbies are concerned, well, there's reading, reading and reading.' It is no wonder then that his films are often inspired by ideas from literature and are full of literary allusions. *Podokkhep*, which according to the director had its genesis in F. Scott Fitzgerald's story 'The Curious Case of Benjamin Button', begins with a quote from Graham Greene's story 'May We Borrow Your Husband': 'At the end … the only love which lasts is the love that has accepted everything … even the sad fact that in the end there is no desire as deep as the simple desire for companionship.' It is this that lends poignancy to Shashanka's (Soumitra Chatterjee) relationship with the five-year-old Trisha, at the core of which lies his loneliness – he has long retired from work, he is a widower and his daughter, Megha (Nandita Das), albeit conscientious and loving, has her own life and career to occupy her.

A couple of early exchanges give an indication of what Shashanka seeks and lacks. His daughter scolds him lovingly for nicking his cheek while shaving. It reverberates in his mind as a voiceover of the 'child' Megha as he stares vacantly at the leisurely rotating ceiling fan when it is time for his afternoon nap. It's a moment filled with the indescribable loss of realizing that one's children have grown up and moved on. The second exchange involves a friend Sunil Bhattacharya. This is the only time in the film till Trisha enters his life – and to an extent even after – that Shashanka actually laughs. The friends play chess, discuss Shombhu Mitra in *Raktakorobi*, fixed deposits and interest rates, the financial losses Sunil has suffered in the recent past, and Gaugin having been a stock broker, at the end of which Sunil has a throwaway line – which you are reminded of only later – about a group of elderly people exercising in the park nearby: '*Bachar ki shawk*' – what a strong desire to live they have.

This exchange with Sunil throws into relief the vacuum in Shashanka's life. Time hangs heavy on his hand till Trisha comes into the picture and literally sweeps him off his aged legs, providing him a second wind. There's a series of delightful exchanges between the two – quarrelling over the TV remote (he wants the news, she wants cartoon); he teaching him to make paper boats and she using the day's newspaper, which he hasn't yet read, to do so; she espying him reaching for a smoke and promptly reporting it; he escorting her to school and gazing lovingly at the cacophony of children at play, all of this culminating in their daylong outing – the park, the tram ride, an ice-cream treat. Shashanka returns home that evening with a long-lost contentment about him only to discover that his friend Sunil has passed away.

In a sequence that plays out largely in silence, Shashanka comments about 'the whole perspective' (of life) coming together only now – the joy of companionship irretrievably offset by death. The camera holds his face, suffused with a mix of myriad emotions, before cutting to father and daughter going over a photo album, Shashanka remembering the mundane minutiae of life as it used to be. In a few brief strokes, Suman Ghosh lays bare what remains of Shashanka's life. Including the potent image of a tree which he distinctly remembers but whose fruit he cannot recall for the life of him ('*adbhut phol hoto laal ronger*' – it bore a strange reddish fruit).

Which cues into the film's climactic sequence, one of great emotional heft: a picnic outing involving Shashanka, Megha, Trisha and Trisha's parents. In a masterstroke, Suman shoots the sequence to the backdrop of Moushumi Bhowmik's eloquent ode to dreams and loss: '*Shopno dekhbo bole*'. Soumitra Chatterjee here provides a masterclass, his face and body language defining regret and consternation – watching Trisha in her father's arms as the lines '*Kothaye shanti paabo bolo kothaye giye*' (tell me where do I find peace) play on the soundtrack. It's a moment filled with a lifetime of longing and regret for the times that are gone. The song continues as Trisha takes Shashanka away, running through the park, with him panting and puffing, barely able to keep his eyes open with the exertion (ironically to the line '*Tai shopno dekhbo boley aami duchokh petechhi*'). It is almost as if it is Shashanka's last stand to hold on to his memories, leading him to the tree in the photograph with the red fruit in full bloom … or does it? As Shashanka goes round and round the tree in wonder and the camera keeps circling him before he collapses, one is left wondering about the nebulous nature of memories.

If *Dwando* fails to evoke these aspects as strongly as *Podokkhep* it is because the central conflict in it pertains to a woman having to decide whether to abort the child she is carrying – which leads only tangentially to the conflict experienced by the irascible Dr Mukherjee (Soumitra Chatterjee). For Sudipta (Ananya Chatterjee), her relationship with Anik (Kaushik Sen) has become a matter of habit over ten years of marriage. She has an affair with a colleague Rana (Samrat Chakraborty) – starting off almost as a dare at an office party ('Only those who risk going too far can possibly find out how far one can go,' the director has Rana quoting T.S. Eliot). When she becomes pregnant, she more or less decides to come clean with Anik, only to have her plans stymied as the latter suffers a brain stroke and has to be operated upon. That is when she lands up at the door of Dr Mukherjee, wanting to know Anik's chances of survival. The child she is carrying is not his, and if he lives, the child has to be aborted. 'In the lie there can be love, in truth never,' she tells Dr Mukherjee.

The films comes into its own only around the hour mark when Dr Mukherjee learns of Sudipta's predicament. He is initially reluctant to meet her and instructs his house-help to tell her, '*Badi nei, moray gechhe.*' (He isn't home, has passed away.) But relents in the face of her perseverance. The remaining thirty minutes are yet another masterclass by the actor. One can only marvel at how he lends musicality to the parts of the brain – 'the tentorium … cerebellum … a pale delicate structure reminding you of the whirl of a veiled dancer' – or equates the delicacy of a brain surgery to poetry, in his words the anatomy of poetry, the poetry of anatomy, quoting Walt Whitman: 'I am the poet of the body, I am the poet of the soul.'

However, Sudipta's predicament lands him in one of his own – how far will his appraisal of Anik's situation lead Sudipta to take the decision of aborting the child. Does either of them have the right to decide on the life of an unborn child? That is when the film delves into the tropes of memory and death as Dr Mukherjee finds himself reminiscing – with the disclaimer 'If I have the permission to indulge in some sentimentality' – about the past, involving his wife Neela. It's as poignant a sequence as any in *Podokkhep* as he describes their efforts at having a child and the agony of holding a still-born in his arms. They had thought of Aripra – the flawless one – as her name, and Suman Ghosh gets the best out of Soumitra as he says: 'Is this the outcome of years of prayers?' It is the only time in his life that he has prayed, says Dr Mukherjee, before the realization dawns on him that life does not halt and he decides to dedicate his life to 'exercising the sentimental proteins of the brain'. There is something strangely affecting in the way Soumitra Chatterjee puts across the agony of reliving his memory and for a moment providing a glimpse of the man behind the grumpy exterior.

Fittingly, given the actor's expertise with recitation, Suman Ghosh ends the film with Soumitra Chatterjee quoting from the Mahabharata: *Na narmayuktam vachanam hinasti na strishu raajan na vivaahakaale/Praanaatyayee sarvadhanaapahaare panchaanrutaanyaahurapaatakaani* – which basically lists the five situations in which telling a lie is not sinful. In what stands testimony to the actor's quest for perfection, Soumitra Chatterjee actually called up Nrishinga Prasad Bhaduri, an Indologist and authority on the epics, to understand the meaning and ensure he had the pronunciation right.

With *Peace Haven* this engagement takes a delectable turn. This, as the director says, was a tribute to his father and uncles, who time and again in their conversations mocked death. Over a mere seventy-five minutes, Suman Ghosh weaves in an experience that is as morbidly funny as it is haunting.

The film begins with a man's death throes on the soundtrack, the ticking of a clock, the wail of an ambulance siren, over a blank screen. His friends Prabhat, Sukumar and Achyut – Paran Bandopadhyay, Soumitra Chatterjee and Arun Mukherjee, respectively, in what is possibly the finest piece of ensemble performance in Bengali cinema in recent years – realize that Pranab's son, Ani, who stays abroad, won't be able to make it in time for the funeral and there is no facility enabling the preservation of the body long enough for the son to return. There are only two mortuaries available, one of which has a problem with refrigeration, while the other, called 'Peace Haven', is overbooked (a VIP politician and film star have laid claim to the only available spaces). Perforce, the last rites are conducted by Ani's friend Raktim, who has one hand glued to a mobile phone at all times.

To forestall the possibilities of such indignity, the friends decide to build a mortuary of their own, towards which end they undertake a surreal journey that affords the film-maker an opportunity to comment on memory, ageing and death. It is in effect a road movie like no other as Ghosh strikes the most delicate of balance between gravity and levity.

Consider, for example, the trio's visit to Peace Haven to check out the facilities. The caretaker, a decrepit old man called Nimai – delightfully played by Suman Ghosh regular Nimai Ghosh – whom one of the friends describes as 'a living dead body', shows them three recesses supposedly holding Mother Teresa, Jyoti Basu and Robi Ghosh. What adds to the absurdity of the sequence is the discussion that follows: all three personalities in the cells are short, while the friends themselves are rather tall. The response from the caretaker – that he could fit them all in one itself if need be – is a hoot. There's also a class system for the alcoves – at Rs 5000, Rs 10000, and Rs 20000 – depending on facilities (teakwood, imported chemicals … is a barber service included in the Rs 20000 bracket, one of the friends asks). Or for that matter, the way they discuss dressing up their dead friend for the final journey – looking for his dentures, draping him in a shawl (advisable, given the heat?).

This segues into a discussion the friends have on whether the feast that precedes and follows their death ought to be vegetarian or non-veg (there's even a tiff between the friends arising from a confusion: is the feast for the opening ceremony of their mortuary or their shraddha), whether to carry designer glasses or the snuff box in the coffins that will hold their bodies till their children arrive for the cremation, whether to employ still photography or videography. All of these delivered deadpan with utmost solemnity.

Complementing the well-thought-out absurdity of these sequences are moments of quiet contemplation, for example, Achyut gazing in passing at the framed footprints of his deceased wife. Or the dreamlike encounter each friend has with aspects of their past – Achyut meeting his wife, wearing the earring and sari he had bought with an increment, who complains about how neglected she felt all her life given his workaholic nature; or Prabhat coming across his father (Paran in a laugh-out-loud double role, taunting his son for planning his own cremation with such meticulousness, imported chemicals and oils and all, while in his time he was just consigned to the poor old khatiya, not even an electric crematorium). In the most eloquent of these interactions, Sukumar finds himself in the middle of a ruin where he stumbles on to his high-school biology class and a discussion on the functioning of the heart, followed by a doctor pronouncing his cancer having spread beyond redemption. ('We are ready for you … it's your turn,' the doctor announces ominously, as Sukumar looks on with something approaching fear.)

This feeling of abject terror in the face of death is reinforced by Achyut's trancelike experience of being part of a funeral procession where he realizes that the body on the bier is his. He keeps running away till he reaches a dead-end (no pun intended) and the only words he can utter to ward death off is: 'I have not had a shave!' In another sequence, Pranab speaks about his encounter with a bat which leads to a discussion on bats facing extinction, which I quote because it so tragically conveys the feeling the old have of having outlived their utility.

> *Achyut*: Do bats have a value in the food chain?
> *Sukumar*: Do you?
> *Achyut*: No. That is why we are on our way to extinction.

All this leads to the film's pièce de resistance, the sequence by the beach bathed in a white light. In a series of fade-ins and fade-outs devoid of dialogue, with just a trumpet sounding a dirge, we see a lighthouse, the sun rising in the horizon, we encounter the characters and elements we have come across in the film – Raktim with his cell phone, the caretaker at Peace Haven, the newspapers and milk pouches accumulating outside Achyut's home, the bat lying dead, a gaggle of children in front of a blackboard, even the dog that has followed the three friends all thorough the road trip (echoing the Pandavas' trip to heaven) and a full-fledged funeral feast. The sequence gives way to Sukumar reciting the lines:

> *Aaj ke bhorer alo e ujjal*
> *Ei jiboner padda patar jol*
> *Tobuo e jol*
> *Kothha theke aashe*
> *Ek nimeshe*
> *Kothaye chole jaaye*

*Bujhechhi aami tomake bhalo beshe*
*Raat phurole podder pataye*

The droplets on the lotus leaf of life sparkles bright
In the light of dawn
Yet no one knows
Where it comes from
And where it disappears in a moment
It dawned on me
As I fell in love with you
At the end of the night
Just like the lotus leaf

Having reached journey's end, the three friends are seen sitting on a bench with the vast expanse of the sea behind them as Achyut asks the question that lies at the heart of the film: '*Ei ze 75 ta bochhor katailam, is equal to ta ki hoilo*' – what have these seventy-years of our lives amounted to. (The director mentions that this is a verbatim reproduction of his uncle Sundar-kaku's observation one afternoon.) Sukumar, by far the most composed of the three friends, breaks down. The camera moves up for a panoramic view of the beach, the dog to the left of the frame, the lighthouse to the right – and no answer to Achyut's query forthcoming. One lives, one accumulates memories, one ages, and death comes as an end.

If I began with *Podokkhep* and end with *Basu Poribar*, it's not just because the films were made in that order but also because the themes that I mention kind of reach an apogee with

*Basu Poribar*. Inspired by James Joyce's *The Dead*, the basic story – a family get-together to celebrate a fiftieth wedding anniversary – provides just the right framework for a journey to exorcise the ghosts of the past. It begins with Pranab's (Soumitra Chatterjee) voiceover of a letter (itself a dead mode in this era of emails, Facetime and WhatsApp), inviting his son Raja (Jisshu Sengupta) and daughter-in-law Roshni (Sreenanda Shankar) to commemorate his fiftieth wedding anniversary with Manjari (Aparna Sen). The words of the letter provide the film with its theme: 'At this age there's nothing much to do but look at the past … reminisce, our days are numbered.'

Though the occasion is festive and everyone – Raja's sister (Rituparna Sengupta) and their relatives Tonu (Koushik Sen) and Pompi (Sudipta Chakraborty) – puts on a bright and happy face, there are enough indications that skeletons abound in the cupboard, aspects that are either not spoken of or are hinted at in hushed tones. There's Tublu, Pranab's nephew, who scrupulously avoids being with his relatives and keeps roaming the abandoned grounds surrounding the palatial mansion 'Komolini'. There's the new bride Roshini who, despite being asked not to, goes exploring the 'purono rajbadi', now a ruin, moss-covered, overgrown with creepers, symbolic of all the memories we want suppressed. The old mansion itself becoming a character, hiding in its nooks and corners secrets that the family prefers to forget with their selective remembrances of happy summers past. In this, the director is aided immensely by another master at work – composer Bickram Ghosh, a regular collaborator with Suman. Bickram's plangent sarod strains as Tublu wanders around the mansion is fittingly elegiac.

However, memories have a way of finding their way through – and Suman Ghosh uses two extraordinary set pieces to unmask the truths that have been buried for decades. In the first, the family gathers around a sofa set and there's a lot of banter as the younger generation goads Manjari and Pranab to talk about their past. This is the past everyone is comfortable about, these are happy memories, though cutaways to Tublu ambling across the grounds and a couple of dialogues cast an ominous shadow. At the outset of the group settling down around the sofa, Manjari says: 'Is there anything that remains hidden after fifty years?' As it turns out, there are. Towards the end of the scene, Raja's sister, going through a troubled marriage, observes wistfully, awed by her parents having stayed together for fifty years: 'There are so many things that stay hidden even after fifty years, no?' Fittingly, the sequence ends with an elderly relative's rendition of '*Aami onek cheye o parini bhulite tomake*' (I haven't been able to forget you despite trying my best) – a song whose relevance reveals itself only towards the end, when one learns of Manjari's secret.

Between this sequence and the other set piece, there are a number of little moments that evoke the shadow memories cast on our lives. The way Manjari fleetingly caresses the do-tara, the conversations around the sweetmeat jalbhora from the well-known Surjo Modok, the brother and sister reminiscing about long-ago summer vacations, and the searing sequence between Kaushik Sen and Rituparna in the room with the hunting trophies where Tonu comes clean about his sexuality. And in all of these there is the overarching sense of people seeking solace in forgetting and life's inability to grant you that.

All of this leads to the climactic set piece at the dinner table which is as fraught as the first one was serene. It begins with a slightly tipsy Pranab, still unaware of the potential the truth has of breaking free, toasting the family, his voice full of pride in his ancestry, the blue blood running through his veins, as he recites a poem by Tagore. But the ghosts of the past will not lie buried any longer, and with Tublu egging them on, the edifice of a carefully nurtured past comes crashing down.

As the rain that has threatened to break all day comes pouring, and Tublu's voice soars over the landscape, each member of the family is left to ponder about what their lives amount to in the larger scheme of things. The film comes to a close with a chastened Pranab's pensive voiceover (written by Soumitra Chatterjee himself in what could be a fitting epigraph to a glittering career), the muted strains of '*Barsan lagi re badariya*' accompanying it: 'Did it rain with this intensity all those years ago? … I do not have the answers any more … But this much I realize today. Howsoever entangled we are in this small circle of our individual lives, it has no bearing on the larger rhythms of nature. A curse from the womb of the past raises its fangs to sting us, reminding us of the eternal truth: that there exists something infinitely larger beyond our personal trials and tribulations. … The patter of the rain makes me experience something deeper than the fragility of ancestry, the fading pride of a nebulous past, and even the crevices in my apparent success.'

The director mentions wanting to convey the essence of James Joyce's philosophy which come alive in the last couple of pages of *The Dead*. "I consider this one of the finest pieces of writing ever in the English language and there was no way I could bring out its essence in Bengali. There were only two people I knew in Bengal who could do that, Shankha Ghosh and Soumitra-kaku. I was thinking of asking another poet I know, when Soumitra-kaku himself said: 'Why don't you let me translate this – if you don't like it, you could throw it away and get someone else to do it.' A couple of days later, he called me home and narrated it to me. That is what we have as the end narration in the film. I have framed his translation."

It's a monologue that captures the essence of the film. The past lives on in us, with all its bittersweet memories. Despite our efforts to look at it through nostalgia-tinted glasses, uncomfortable truths have a way of seeping through. And the dead often cast a long shadow over the present, the living. Fifty years is just a matter of time… and yet, not quite…

# 1

# 15 November 2020

Sunday. In my home in Miami, I woke up to numerous messages from friends in India conveying the news of Soumitra Chatterjee's (Kaku from hereon) demise. I remember reading those condolence messages and going back to bed – clearly not knowing how to react. Lying down I digested the fact that he was no more. Willing myself to leave the bed after a while, I turned on ABP Ananda Live to watch the news. Soumitra-kaku's last journey, to the crematorium, was being telecast. Despite the pandemic, thousands of people had gathered to pay their respects. Leading them was the chief minister of Bengal, Mamata Banerjee. I sat transfixed, devoid of any feelings, seeing those images on my iPad.

A little later, my two daughters, Maya and Leela – seven and five, respectively – came to my room and hugged me. My wife told them that 'Sonar Kella Dadu' was no more and hence Papa was sad. Their gesture was very touching – just the kind of solace I needed at that juncture. I need to mention here that a couple of months back they had seen *Sonar Kella*, the Feluda film directed by Satyajit Ray and starring Soumitra-kaku, and loved it. They had sent a lovely video message to Soumitra-kaku conveying their joy. In return, Soumitra-kaku had sent an equally warm message profusely 'thanking' them. That was the genesis of the term 'Sonar Kella Dadu'. After they left me alone, I kept on looking at the visuals on my iPad. There was a close shot of his daughter Poulomi caressing Soumitra-kaku's face before he was carried away.

Towards the last years of his working life, he used to take a post-lunch nap before he resumed shooting. My team would make special arrangements so that he could rest peacefully. Once we were ready to commence shoot after lunch, I would go to his room and wake him up. He looked so peaceful sleeping, I used to feel bad doing so. Somehow seeing him prone before his final journey I was reminded of that. As if he was waiting to be called for his post-lunch shoot. I could sense a pent-up grief within myself. *The Telegraph* in Kolkata had requested me to write an obituary. I decided to take that up. I am glad that I did so since it was a cathartic experience at that point. Here is what I wrote:

### *'Soumitra Chatterjee: Renaissance Man's Solace*[2]

Renaissance man, an ideal that developed in Renaissance Italy, refers to a man who can do all things if he wills. The ideal embodied the basic tenets of Renaissance humanism, which considered man the centre of the universe, limitless in his capacities for development, and led to the notion that men should try to embrace all knowledge and develop their own capacitates as fully as possible. In terms of the great Bengalis that have lived over the years, this term was used for such specific qualities in men during the Bengal Renaissance. The use of the term specifically for 'men' is surely suspect but I mean it in terms of the idea of the qualities mentioned. In recent times, one thinks of people like Amartya Sen,

2 Published in *The Telegraph,* 16 November 2020.

*Basu Poribar*

Satyajit Ray, Soumitra Chatterjee and Aparna Sen who exhibit such qualities. I was indeed fortunate to be closely associated with Soumitra-kaku as an actor in five of my films and then subsequently as my friend, philosopher and guide. Though he is renowned as an internationally acclaimed film actor, I think that is too narrow a space to relegate him to. He was one of the last cultural icons of Bengal who exhibited his intrinsic humanism through his writings, his paintings, his theatre and of course his film performances. That encapsulates the true 'Soumitra Chatterjee'.

I first met Soumitra-kaku during the shoot of one of his films *Dekha* which was directed by Goutam Ghose. I still vividly remember my first impression of seeing the great man at Aurora Studio in North Kolkata. This was in 2000 when I was a PhD student in the US and was contemplating an alternate career as a film-maker. I could not believe my eyes that the person in front of me was the same person who had enamoured countless fans in such seminal films as *Charulata*, *Apur Sansar*, the Feluda films, *Jhinder Bondi*, *Wheel Chair* and many more. I remember that for many days I could not muster up the courage to go up to him and introduce myself.

Five years later, when I decided to make my first film *Podokkhep* with him as the lead along with Nandita Das, I approached him again. To my utter joy he loved the script and agreed to be a part of my film. *Podokkhep* went on to win two National awards including the Best Actor for Soumitra Chatterjee. Thus started my journey with him and later I often laughed with him about the fact that I built my career on his shoulders.

Since then, apart from the shoot days, there were countless long addas with him – topics ranging from literature, history, cricket, Satyajit Ray to the Masai tribes of Africa. He was like a walking encyclopedia on everything. The thing which struck me the most was his immense curiosity to learn new things. He was perhaps the most restless mind that I have ever encountered, wanting to know about apparently trivial things in detail, hence his love of books. He was my book buddy. Each time I came to Kolkata I brought with me books for Soumitra-kaku. Likewise, he would refer many books to me which I diligently read. The literary exchange would end in countless hours of discussion.

Over the course of many years, his zest for work was distinctive, even under extremely trying times. I particularly remember two instances where I was stunned to see his composure. After his grandson Rono was involved in an almost fatal accident a few years back I could not fathom how Soumitra-kaku would accept that. When I went to his house after the incident, I did not know how to face him. When I entered his room, I saw him engrossed in a different world altogether. Work was his solace. Again, last year when he was admitted in the hospital for some major illness, I was in Mumbai. When I went to Kolkata, I was apprehensive about what condition I would find him in. But when I entered his bungalow, the security guard told me that he was in the outhouse. I quietly went there and saw him splashing paint on a canvas – again engrossed in his own world. Creating art from the depths of despair was his way out of despondency.

Today I want to confess a constant fear that I have had for the last few years. Whenever I went to his house during the last couple of years, after our adda he used to come outside to see me off. Even though I repeatedly asked him not to, he would insist and always said, '*O kichhu hobena.*' (Nothing will happen.) When I got into my car and turned back, I would see him waving at me as my car drove away from him. That image touched me each time. I was afraid of not having him like a parent, of him not being there for me. I feel the same today … I am driving away from him in my journey of life while he keeps waving at me, slowly fading away. I know he is there, still waving.

# 2

# Meeting the Legend

I grew up in the 1980s, in a place called Rishra, a suburb of Kolkata. My father was an employee at ICI (Imperial Chemical Industries) and we stayed at the company quarters there. India was a vastly different country at the time. Though television had arrived in India in the previous decade, it caught on only with the advent of colour during the Asian Games in 1982. But even a black-and-white TV set was the preserve of a privileged few. Not every family had one – we, for example, did not have television in our home until the late 1980s.

That gave rise to a quaint custom – one of the era's indelible memories: all those who did not have TV would go to a neighbour's house to watch. We would often tell our parents, "I am going to Sriram's house to watch *Chitrahaar*", or even spend the entire day at someone's place to watch Test cricket. The neighbour meanwhile carried on their daily activities, unfazed by the fact that someone was sitting in the living room watching TV. Those were the days of Doordarshan. And Doordarshan primarily meant news bulletins, *Chitrahaar*, *Chiching Faak* and the feature films which were shown on Saturdays (Bengali) and Sundays (Hindi).

I remember we were allowed to watch Bengali feature films but not the Hindi ones. Hindi films (the term Bollywood was still years away from becoming part of our lexicon) were considered a bad influence on impressionable minds, the common refrain of elders being that if you watched Hindi films, you were beyond redemption. But given our youth, any such embargo only fuelled our curiosity and with it the urge to disregard the ban. As someone who teaches economics, I would compare it to a demand created through repressed supply.

Call it the lure of the prohibited – but the greater the restrictions placed on watching them, the more the fascination with Hindi cinema and its stars. Those were the heydays of Amitabh Bachchan and Mithun Chakraborty. As with most kids our age I was not an exception. I was more interested in films like *Don* and *Disco Dancer* than anything Bengali cinema was producing. Since my parents would not take me to the theatres to watch Hindi films, I often accompanied my elder brother and his friends. The excitement on hearing Amitabh Bachchan's cult dialogue in *Don*, "*Don ko pakadna mushkil hi nahi, namumkin hain*", or to experience an entire cinema hall erupt in *seetees* (whistles) when Mithun appeared in the song *"I am a disco dancer"* was a different high altogether compared to the sedate Bengali films like *Krishna Sudama* and *Arun Barun Kiranmala* which my mother took us to.

Of course, one must remember that mainstream Bengali cinema was going through a lull at the time. Uttam Kumar had passed away in 1980 and ever since Bengali cinema was struggling to regain its lost glory. After Uttam Kumar's demise, actors like Soumitra Chatterjee, Ranjit Mullick, Samit Bhanja, Sandhya Roy, Mahua Roychowdhury and others featured in some interesting films but nothing compared to what came out of Mumbai.

I must confess that Soumitra Chatterjee did not make any mark on my young adolescent mind apart from the roles he played as Feluda. *Sonar Kella* from the previous decade, and then *Joy Baba Felunath*, really left a strong impression on me – like they did on an entire generation of young people – but that was just about it. I remember that Satyajit Ray's *Ghare Baire* released in 1984 but we were not allowed to watch it since it was considered '*boroder chhobi*' (a film for adults only). Middle-class families at the time had a clearly demarcated line between what was suitable for the young to watch and what wasn't. The kiss between its protagonists Sandip (Soumitra-kaku) and Bimala (Swatilekha Sengupta) put *Ghare Baire* firmly in the second category and was enough to render it forbidden. *Kony* released around then and was a super hit but we did not get tickets for any show. The only tickets available were in 'black' – the phenomenon where touts sold tickets at a significant markup. We were not allowed to purchase tickets from 'blackers' on both financial and ethical grounds. It is only much later in life that I watched *Kony* and Soumitra-kaku's marvellous performance in it. But as mentioned before, it was Amitabh-Mithun and the rest of Hindi cinema that drove our dreams and fantasies. Incidentally, who would have imagined that a couple of decades later I would direct Mithun Chakraborty and Soumitra Chatterjee in a film? More on that later.

It was only at Presidency College, where I was a student of economics from 1991 to 1994, that the first inklings of the phenomenon called Soumitra Chatterjee entered my mind space. I particularly remember two films which released at the time that made a strong impact on me: *Wheel Chair* and *Atanka*, both directed by Tapan Sinha. Though *Atanka* had released earlier in the mid-1980s, I watched it on TV. I thought that Soumitra-kaku's performance in these films were amongst the best in his impressive oeuvre. And, of course, while at Presidency I discovered the significance of Satyajit Ray's films. It was while I was at college that Ray passed away. There were huge crowds to pay him their last respects. And

Soumitra-kaku looking at Ray lying in repose at Nandan was one of the era's haunting images. I was reminded of that watching Soumitra-kaku's final journey.

So it was at college that I revisited the Ray greats once more and along with that discovered Soumitra Chatterjee. It was also around this time that film-making started to attract me. From my initial adoration of film stars, my interest and fascination slowly started to shift to film directors. I began to follow the works of Satyajit Ray, Shyam Benegal, Aparna Sen, Goutam Ghose and many other significant film-makers of that era.

I must admit that there were certain pretensions too. There were films one was 'supposed' to like and hence we used to go with the tide. Looking back, I remember that I watched Goutam Ghose's *Padma Nadir Majhi* and Shyam Benegal's *Suraj ka Saatwan Ghora* without really understanding what it was that made them special. However, I did not have the confidence to admit that. On the contrary the film which genuinely fuelled my fascination to become a film-maker was Mani Ratnam's *Roja*. I watched it with friends at Nandan and could immediately decipher the greatness of the director and also the music director, a new guy named A.R. Rahman.

I went to Cornell for my PhD in economics in 1996. While doing my PhD, I started taking film courses in the film department there. I was exposed to not only the great films of legends like Ingmar Bergman, Akira Kurosawa and Federico Fellini, but also experimental films by the likes of Maya Deren, Stan Brakhage and others that made me realize the potency of films as a medium. It slowly dawned on me that this was a profession that interested me more than my main vocation, namely, economics. It was then that I thought of attending a film shoot in India since I was pretty sure that I wanted to make films in my own country. I called up Goutam Ghose from the US to find out when he was shooting his next film and whether I could be on set to watch the filming process. Let me take a minor detour to explain how I knew Goutam Ghose in the first place.

Many years ago, before coming to Cornell for my PhD, I faced a crossroad in life. I wanted to be a film-maker but at the same time I had just got admission for a PhD program in economics at Cornell University. Of course, for my family the choice was obvious but the youthful rebel in me thought there was little doubt that being a film-maker was my calling in life. Just to confirm this I gathered all my courage and called the director who had first sown the seeds of film mania in me. I say this because watching a film of his on television had a huge impact on me.

In the 1980s, Doordarshan used to show award-winning films on TV. Somehow, we found those boring, not necessarily because of the subject matter but because they were always dark (visually) and made intentionally difficult to grasp – or so we thought. One afternoon, while casually watching TV, a scene caught my attention. A poor villager comes to Kolkata for work. He loses the only contact address he has on a chit of paper in a crowded railway station. His frantic search, his helplessness, his anxiety were being brilliantly portrayed by the actor. It bowled me over. I sat down to watch more. The film just gripped me and what I saw subsequently – the river-crossing scene with the pigs – impacted me so deeply that the first seeds of understanding the power of cinema were permanently etched in me. The film was Goutam Ghose's *Paar* and the actor was none other than the great Naseeruddin Shah.

This was many years before the incident that I am going to narrate. I now took out the phone book and called Goutam Ghose.

He was kind enough to meet me but what followed in the meeting left me deeply disappointed. Rather than encouraging me to follow his path I distinctly remember what he said. "You see, Suman, film-making is a very risky career. Since you have got into one of the best universities of the world, I would advise you to go to Cornell, and if you have it in you follow up film-making later. Don't give up this opportunity. Students all over the world would give their right arm to study in a place like that."

I came back from his Golpark apartment with a deep sense of resentment against him. I had no other choice. I did go to Cornell. Only years later did I realize what a mature bit of advice he had given me. Alongside my PhD curriculum I took my film-making courses, and five years later I called Goutam Ghose again and asked him to allow me to be a part of his film. I had diligently followed his advice, now it was payback time.

Goutam Ghose was making a film called *Dekha* and he allowed me to be an observer. To my utmost delight the protagonist in that film was being played by none other than Soumitra Chatterjee. I still remember the first time I saw him. The shooting was at Aurora Studio in North Kolkata. To see my Feluda, my Apu, my Amal, my Mayurbahon in front of me was a strange feeling. In my mind the man was a part of folklore … more fictional than flesh and blood. I just kept staring at him. Hopefully no one in the shoot saw my trancelike state.

I remember one day after an exceptionally fantastic shot I went to him and very timidly told him how much I liked his performance in that particular take. It was a scene between Soumitra-kaku and Indrani Haldar, with the latter playing an editor of a little magazine who is enchanted with Soumitra-kaku's poetry. When she tries to reach out emotionally to Kaku's character he starts behaving rudely with her, clearly as a defence mechanism but

*Podokkhep*

also to test her endurance. The way he delivered his dialogue in the third take conveyed that feeling aptly. When I complimented him, he looked at me and said, "Do you know why this particular take was better?"

Honestly, I didn't.

He then told me, "My guru Sisir Bhaduri used to say, 'Acting is all about pause. How long you pause between words and sentences, whether you will pause or not … all of this is what constitutes acting.' In this particular take, my rhythm and detailing of the pauses were perfect." These were the first exchanges I had with Soumitra-kaku and that was even before we were introduced to each other. To be honest, during the shoot of *Dekha* I hardly had the courage to go up to him and talk. Such was the level of awe. I attended the shoot regularly and just watched him act. I used to listen to the conversations and addas on set with the other cast and crew apart from Goutam-da – Paran Bandopadhyay, Anjan Dutt, Indrani Haldar, Debashree Roy and others. The conversations ranged from both serious discussions on films of Mrinal Sen and Satyajit Ray to light banter, for example, the menu at lunch for the day. There was so much warmth in Goutam-da's unit that it felt like a family. I instinctively felt like I belonged in this world of cinema.

This was in 2000 and I was still a PhD student at Cornell. I came back to the US after my summer holidays. Soon after I completed my PhD and embarked upon my first venture, a documentary on Amartya Sen. Sen was my academic grandfather, in the sense that one of my PhD advisors at Cornell was the renowned economist Kaushik Basu, who had been Sen's PhD student at the London School of Economics in the early 1970s. Given my background in economics and films, Sen was comfortable about allowing me to film the documentary. It is interesting that subsequently in my two professions, economics and films, Sen and Soumitra-kaku became my gurus in life.

For the next few years, I remained busy completing the documentary while at the same time fulfilling my academic duties as an assistant professor in Mexico. During my visits to India, I kept in touch with Soumitra-kaku. As I got to know him, I was intrigued about the man. He was not just an actor of repute but his knowledge and curiosity towards so many things fascinated me. He was an ardent admirer of Amartya Sen and his scholarship. I remember him asking so many questions about Amartya Sen and on economics since, not being a student of economics, he felt he was unable to truly appreciate the work of Sen.

It was around 2003-04 that I decided to embark upon my first feature film. The film was based on the character of a retiree who lives with his daughter and their house help who is more than that, almost a family member. The crux of the story was based on the relationship of the protagonist, the retiree played by Soumitra-kaku, with a little girl who is his neighbour. As the narrative proceeds we see Shashanka (the name of the character) transform to a child – metaphorically representing the lifecycle of a human being getting back to the womb. This was wonderfully represented in Scott Fitzgerald's story 'The Curious Case of Benjamin Button'. I had written the protagonist with Soumitra-kaku in mind and the other main characters would be Nandita Das as his daughter and the great Sabitri Chatterjee as the house help. I remember how I was subconsciously inspired by Ingmar Bergman's *Wild Strawberries* in delineating Sabitri Chatterjee's character and based it on the character of Agda (Jullan Kindahl), the housekeeper to Victor David Sjöström's Professor Isak Borg.

Even after making nine feature films, I have not been able to surmount one problem: Whenever I write a script, I need to have a face attached to a given character to get a better hold of the characterization. The problem with that is I am not sure whether the actor I have in mind might be willing to be a part of the film. I must say that I have lucked out on that aspect till now – whether with Mithun Chakraborty, Konkona Sen Sharma or Aparna Sen.

At the time, Nandita Das was an international star who had featured in several international and Hindi films. I did not know how to convince her to do a Bengali film and that too my debut. Fortunately, Soumitra-kaku was my trump card. By that time Soumitra-kaku had read the script and was on board. I met Nandita in New York and discovered that she was extremely eager to work with the legend. So, the fact that Soumitra-kaku was already on board made my task of convincing her to play his daughter in the film easy. Thus started my film journey, riding on Soumitra-kaku's shoulders.

I started shooting *Podokkhep* (Footsteps) in 2005. I would be lying if I said that I did not feel intimidated about working with such a legend. But during preproduction and the first few days of shoot it was clear that he was a person so dedicated to his craft that all the usual concerns of a first-time director working with him would not be an issue. I remember one thing he told me before the start of the shoot which I adhere to even now. "Look, Suman," he said, "this is your first film. You will soon find out that whatever your vision, there will be many obstacles on the way. You will be told that this or that thing is not available, actors will create problems, there will be financial worries and a host of other issues. But your job is to stick to your vision. At the end of the film even if you achieve 70 per cent of what you set out to do, you should consider it a success. I don't want to scare you but it is always good to be cautious. When people see the film on screen nobody will care about what you went through. What appears on the screen will be the truth."

Thinking back, I realize how valuable that piece of advice was. You enter a shoot as if in a war zone and you have to emerge victorious with your vision intact in the face of many obstacles. Thus began my journey with Soumitra-kaku.

# Interlude

## Shaukat and Soumitra Chatterjee

Shaukat drives my car when I come to Kolkata. We have a wonderful relationship and I have come to know that he awaits my return to Kolkata eagerly. For the past few years, he used to pick-up and drop-off Soumitra Chatterjee from his house in Golf Green whenever I had my long adda sessions (usually at Saturday Club) with Soumitra-kaku.

Last year after Soumitra-kaku passed away, I went to Kolkata in December. After our initial exchanges, Shaukat remarked, "Achha, oi je bhodrolok ke ami Golf Green theke tultam uni ki bikkhyato lok chhilen?" (The gentleman whom I used to pick up from Golf Green ... was he a famous man?)

I said, "Why do you ask?"

He replied, "Uni mara jaoar pawr shara Kolkatai hoarding e sroddha janachhey ... tai bujhlam bikhyato lok chhilen." (There were hoardings all over Kolkata after he died. That's how I came to know he was a famous man.)

After a brief pause, he continued. "Kintu khub bhalo lok chhilen. Amar shonge onek golpo korten. Bondhutto hoye gechhilo." (But he was a good man. We used to chat a lot. He became my friend.)

*I found the story incredibly touching. Here was Shaukat forming a friendship with Soumitra Chatterjee. He had never told me about this, neither had Soumitra-kaku. I did not ask Shaukat what they talked about. It is their personal relationship. I have no right to intrude. I just replied, "Hyan, khub bhalo lok chhilen." (Yes, he was indeed a good man.) Shaukat does not have to know how famous Soumitra Chatterjee was. That's not important.*

While waiting for the lighting to be done on the sets of *Peace Haven*, Soumitra-kaku made this sketch and gifted it to me. He was an incredible painter, as I discovered in the course of my interactions with him.

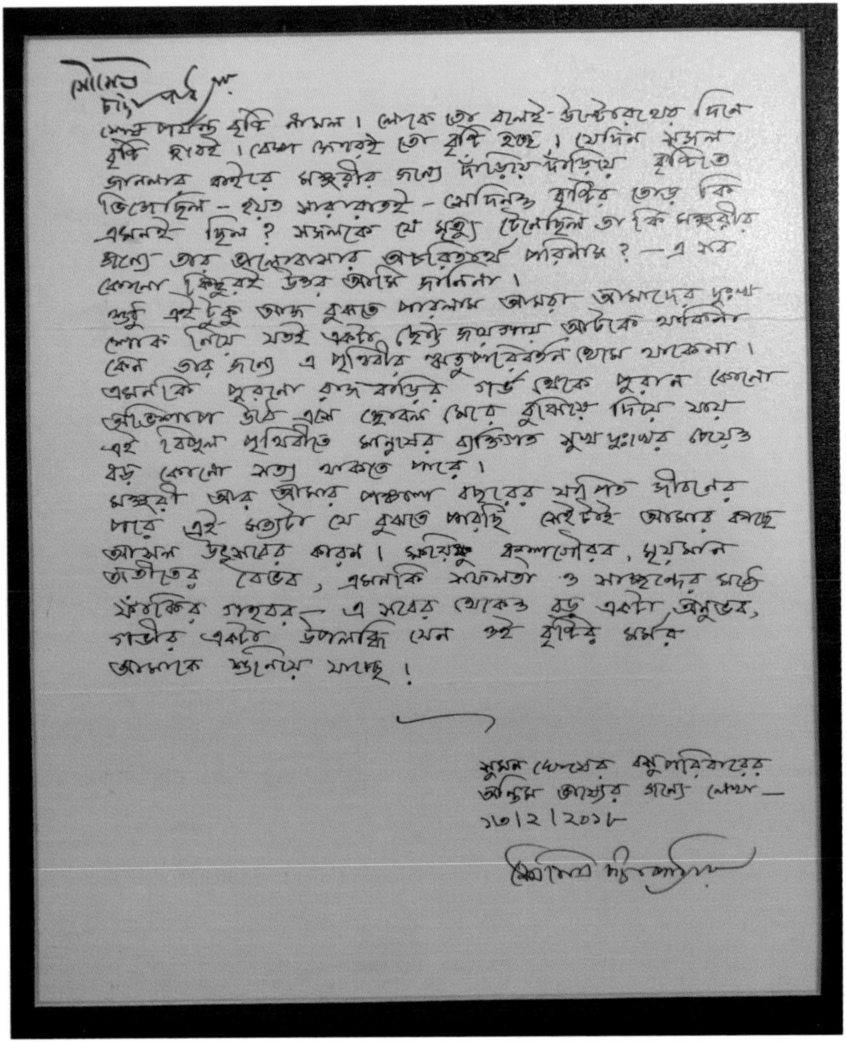

শেষ পর্যন্ত বৃষ্টি নামল। লোকে তো বলেই - উল্টোরথের দিনে বৃষ্টি হবেই। বেলা ভোরেই তো বৃষ্টি হচ্ছে। যেদিন সজল জানলার বাইরে মঞ্জরীর জন্যে দাঁড়িয়ে দাঁড়িয়ে বৃষ্টিতে ভিজেছিল — হয়ত সারারাতই — সেদিনও বৃষ্টির তোড় কি এমনই ছিল? সজলকে যে মৃত্যু টেনেছিল তা কি মঞ্জরীর জন্যে তার ভালোবাসার অচরিতার্থ পরিণাম? — এ সব কোনো কিছুরই উত্তর আমি জানিনা।

শুধু এইটুকু আজ বুঝতে পারলাম আমরা আমাদের দুঃখ শোক নিয়ে যতই একটা ছোট্ট জায়গায় আটকে থাকিনা কেন তার জন্যে এ পৃথিবীর ঋতুপরিবর্তন থেমে থাকেনা। এমনকি পুরনো বাড়ির গর্ভ থেকে পুরান কোনো অভিশাপ উঠে এসে ছোবল মেরে বুঝিয়ে দিয়ে যায় এই বিপুল পৃথিবীতে মানুষের ব্যক্তিগত সুখ দুঃখের চেয়েও বড় কোনো সত্য থাকতে পারে।

মঞ্জরী আর আমার পঞ্চাশ বছরের যাপিত জীবনের পারে এই সত্যটা যে বুঝতে পারছি সেইটেই আমার কাছে আসল উৎসবের কারণ। সম্পূর্ণ বংশগৌরব, দুর্মূল্য অতীতের বৈভব, এমনকি সফলতা ও সাচ্ছন্দ্যের মেকি ঝকমকির [illegible] — এ সবের থেকেও বড় একটা অনুভব, গভীর একটা উপলব্ধি যেন ওই বৃষ্টির মর্মর আমাকে শুনিয়ে যাচ্ছে!

সুমন ঘোষের বসু পরিবারের
অন্তিম ভাষ্যের জন্যে লেখা —
১৩/২/২০১৮

সৌমিত্র চট্টোপাধ্যায়

The final monologue from *Basu Poribar* that Soumitra-kaku translated from the last two pages of James Joyce's *The Dead*. It gave me the perfect ending for the film which was inspired by Joyce's novella.

Soumitra-kaku was a child at heart. In my daughters Maya and Leela, he had two playmates about eighty years younger. Here, they are at their 'Sonar Kella Dadu's' house, creating their own fantasy land, in the process ransacking his living room.

Maya, Leela and my wife Vidhi at Soumitra-kaku's house.

Guess Who Came to Lunch! Soumitra-kaku was gracious enough to visit us at our home over lunch. A memorable day for every member of my family.

Soumitra-kaku with Nandita Das and Mrinal Sen at the premiere of *Podokkhep* at Nandan.

The last of the Renaissance Men of Bengal, Amartya Sen and Soumitra Chatterjee, at the screening of my documentary, *The Argumentative Indian*, at Nandan in 2018. Both epitomize a culture and intellect that is sadly no longer to be found in Bengal.

On the sets of *Basu Poribar*. He had performed the emotional climactic sequence brilliantly, reciting Tagore, but I was not happy with the teardrops that rolled down his cheeks. Here I am telling him that and explaining why. Soumitra-kaku understood and we shot again. This time for a perfect take.

On location, *Peace Haven*, an exploration of death, a subject on which Soumitra-kaku and I had a number of discussions. I even conceptualized a bizarre idea for another film, which he was very enthused about. Unfortunately, we never got to putting it together.

On the sets of *Dwando*, in a mansion in North Calcutta. The sequence involved an intricate lighting job and Soumitra-kaku was intrigued by the nuanced lighting. He looked through the camera and complimented the DOP, Barun Mukherjee, for the same.

A still from the last section of *Dwando*. The colour and texture of the house coat Soumitra-kaku wears involved a lot of deliberation given the character attributes and the hue we wanted to shoot the sequence in.

Aparna Sen and Soumitra-kaku on the sets of *Basu Poribar*. Thanks to a malfunctioning generator, we had lost power. Soumitra-kaku was preparing for the scene and going over his dialogues with the script. Aparna Sen immediately switched on her phone torch and told him, "You read. I will hold the light."

# 3

# An Actor Prepares

'An actor is a messenger entrusted with conveying something without distorting or damaging it.' – Naseeruddin Shah

In a wonderful essay titled 'What Makes for Truth in Acting?', Naseeruddin Shah wrote, "The dictionary meaning of the word 'act' is not 'to pretend' or 'to play different characters' or 'disguise oneself' or 'emote' but quite simply 'to do'. Those who aren't aware of this (and that includes an astonishing number of actors I have met) will consider it paradoxical to talk of honesty in an activity that is naturally taken to be an artifice. Yet, even they will admit that the elusive quality of truth is the holy grail of every thinking actor's journey and of their own expectations from the actor."

I have been asked many times about Soumitra Chatterjee's method of acting. The reason I quote Naseeruddin Shah is because what he says succinctly describes what Soumitra-kaku did. He was the perfect 'messenger'. He was often called a 'director's actor'. Basically, he never considered himself bigger than the film or the director's vision. He submitted himself completely to the director's vision and conveyed that vision 'without distorting or damaging it'. I believe that the best performances emerge when the eye of the director becomes the eye of the actor. When it comes to the relationship between a director and an actor in the making of a film, it is like walking together, searching together and becoming one. Hence, what Soumitra-kaku always tried was to understand the director (both as an artist and as a person), his or her vision, and then travel together, wired to the director's vision, in step with that. He then had to just 'do' or 'be'.

I cannot assign a standard template about how he prepared for each role but what I can do is discuss my interactions with him for each of the films that we worked on together. Interactions both before and in the process of making the film. That will give an idea of how he prepared for each role and in turn how he contributed to the films he worked in, beyond his role as an actor.

**Back to the womb: *Podokkhep* (2006)**

This was my first feature film. And with all the bravado of a naïve debutant I had dared to cast none other than Soumitra Chatterjee. After completing the script, I called him up and told him about my film. He wanted to read the script. I was in the US and so I sent the script to him by post. I waited, holding my breath, for almost a month for his reaction. When I called him up soon after he had read the script, I was elated to know that he loved it. He had some comments and observations which he said he would like to discuss in person rather than on phone. He enquired about the timing of my shoot and when I intended to come to Kolkata. That was it. Soumitra Chatterjee was on board and now I had to take the plunge.

I was still an assistant professor in my university and that implied I did not have tenure. For an academician in the US, 'tenure' is a big deal. Basically, based on your research output and teaching credentials, the university decides whether to make your job permanent or not. If one does not succeed in getting tenure, one has to leave the job and look for other options. I had decided to take the risk.

To say that I felt a mild trepidation about working with Soumitra Chatterjee would be an understatement. I remember the first time I went to his place and gave him my brief. I told him about the journey of his character. That this man was in his seventies but as the story progresses, he slowly becomes like a child, a change brought about by his interaction with the five-year-old kid he befriends. At some point his mannerisms will become indistinguishable from that of the child.

Interacting with him, I realized that he needed intellectual stimulation to prepare for a role. I could sense what he was getting at. Since I was also the writer of the film, he wanted to know what my vision of the film and his character was. Has it been influenced by real events, or was it based on someone, or from literature? That way he could be on the same wavelength as the writer-director and understand what exactly I wanted. Remember, this was my first film with him and he also needed to know me as a person. That would give him an idea of my aesthetics, my values and my inspirations. He needed to imbibe those aspects within him to carry out my vision. In fact, I follow this with all my lead actors. I sincerely believe that the director and the actor should know each other very well beyond just the story and the script in order to bring about the confluence which ultimately leads to a wholesome piece of work.

With that in mind I gave him F. Scott Fitzgerald's 'The Curious Case of Benjamin Button' which had a similar arc where the protagonist ages in reverse. I also told him about a disease called progeria which has similar symptoms. The curious mind in him wanted to know more about the disease and so I provided him medical literature on the same. Then I started discussing with him about physical gestures. The first thing I remember asking him was whether he could change his gait. His iconic walk was of course very popular in Bengali cinema but I told him that this character did not need the 'Soumitra Chatterjee walk'. In the course of our conversation, I started becoming comfortable – here was a man with whom I could communicate freely; his iconic status was not a hindrance.

We also discussed small gestures children make and the psychological basis for these to include in his mannerisms. I told him that many of the character traits belonged to my father who was approximately his age. Observing my father interact with my four-year-old nephew was such a delight and many of the scenes in the film were lifted directly from those interactions. I remember my father watching the TV news every evening and my nephew switching the news channel to the cartoon channel and the subsequent fights between them. Most of the time my nephew emerged victorious and I could see my father sitting next to him, watching cartoon with a grumpy face. Seeing that I used to wonder – who is the kid here? Soumitra-kaku performed this scene to perfection in *Podokkhep* with Sabitri Chatterjee (playing their house help) telling him in exasperation that the little girl was the 'kid', not him, and he should not forget that and behave like one himself.

In fact, after my father retired, I had observed him engaging with issues which other people would find trivial. However, with age (or as with children) that is what fascinates them. Hence, I discussed a lot about my father with Soumitra-kaku. I told him stories, many of which were unrelated to the script directly, but I am sure Soumitra-kaku picked up cues from those stories.

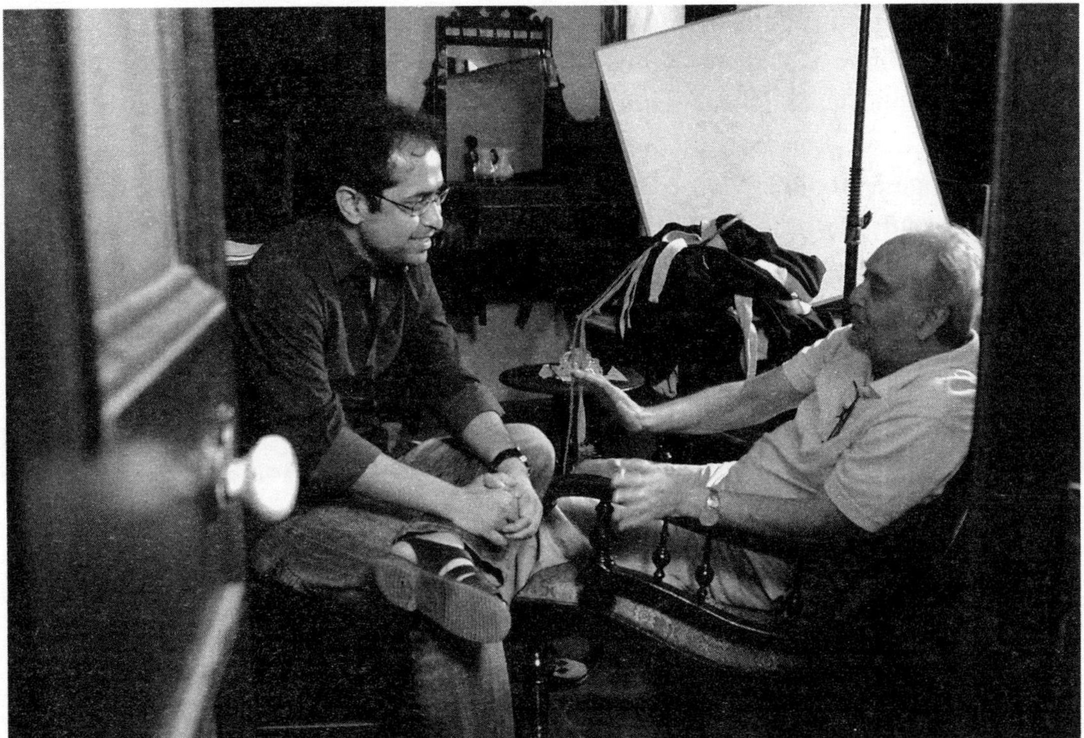

Suman Ghosh and Soumitra Chatterjee during a break in shoot

If one watches the film closely, in the early sequences his portrayal is of a quintessential retired person. Playing chess with his friend, trying to restructure the house, bothering about his fixed deposits and being overprotective about his grown-up daughter. A distinct change comes over Shashanka (the name of the character in the film) after his five-year-old neighbour rushes into his apartment, chased by her mother. It is as if Trisha (the child) turns his otherwise sedate life topsy-turvy. Shashanka finds a new purpose which gives him a fresh lease of life – taking her to school, going out for 'dates' with her, gardening with her. His character traits also slowly become indistinguishable from that of Trisha's, and at one point his daughter becomes worried when she finds him lying on the floor, fascinated by a procession of ants in their bedroom. I remember I used to do that when I was a child. I had a feeling of wonder at the life of ants and used to spend hours watching them. For some reason, that made it into my script.

As the story progresses, we see him becoming more and more childlike, completely unaware of his deteriorating heart condition. Eventually, his daughter becomes more like the father figure to her elderly father. Note how towards the end when he is at the clinic for a check-up, it is Nandita who is scolding him for surreptitiously smoking (in a touching inversion of roles from the beginning where it was Shashanka who would reprimand her like a father).

This particular sequence also highlighted how a great actor makes the optimal use of a prop. I had given him a magazine – the kind one finds at a doctor's clinic. The way he fidgeted with the corner of a page from the magazine added layers to the sequence, giving an insight into his troubled mind, his childish impatience. I do this quite often with actors. For example, in *Kadambari*, there's a scene where Robi Thakur and his wife, Mrinalini, go on an outing soon after their marriage. Kadambari (Konkona Sen Sharma) enters their room which was till recently her space for shared moments with Robi. There's a song playing in the background. As a prop I had left a sari on the bedstead. I didn't tell Konkona anything to do with it. In a brilliant improvisation, Konkona smells the sari – that belongs to Mrinalini – conveying not only her desolation but also the element of sexual jealousy so subtly. Soumitra-kaku achieved something similar with his gesture with the magazine. And immediately afterwards, as they leave the clinic, there's another action he engages in that eloquently communicates his state of mind. All of us are aware of how children often have the habit of scratching at a wall as they walk alongside one. Soumitra-kaku replicated that gesture as he walked away from the clinic, effortlessly conveying that juvenile aspect.

In an earlier scene in the film, he made great use of another intelligent prop. This is when he returns from an outing with Trisha and learns of his friend's death. I had given him a *shankho* (a conch) as a prop. The *shankho* has certain spiritual/religious connotations, and Soumitra-kaku, reflecting on the day he had spent with the little girl and absorbing the news of his friend's death, delivered the entire scene playing with the *shankho* in his hands. It adds layers to the scene.

By the time Trisha leaves for the US with her family, there is almost nothing left for him. In the final scene, the way he sobs lying on the hospital bed, couched in a foetal position, symbolizes his 'death'. The portrayal of this arc lay at the heart of the film and that was Soumitra-kaku's challenge.

The fact that a film is almost never shot chronologically made his job even tougher. He had to maintain the character graph as per my brief. For example, we would often shoot a scene from the end of the film first for logistical reasons and he had to remember where his acting arc would be at that stage. I could sense his diligence as he made intense preparations. In his copy of the script, he noted down every detail in excruciating detail – what scene we were shooting and what was the character like at that stage. I really wish I had collected his script after the shoot. Especially since this remains his only National Award performance.

I distinctly remember the first day of shoot. We were shooting at the Dhakuria Lake in South Kolkata. Soumitra-kaku and the legendary theatre personality Bibhash Chakraborty were the artists. The scene required them to play chess. I was extremely nervous about calling 'action' for the first time in my life. And the fact that a huge crowd was watching the shoot, to my mind watching my insecurity, made it even more tense for me. Just before I was going to say 'action', Soumitra-kaku stopped the proceedings. He came up to me and said, "Suman, this is the first shot of your career. I just wanted to wish you a long and successful journey ahead. Don't be tense. Just enjoy the flow." It was such a beautiful gesture. He could discern what was going through in my mind. It calmed me down a lot and touched my heart to the core. The journey continued, with that man at the forefront.

Another fact I found striking was how wonderful he was as a co-actor. He formed a long-lasting relationship with Nandita Das. When we were shooting for *Podokkhep*, Nandita was writing the script of her debut film *Firaaq*, starring Naseeruddin Shah. I realized then that Soumitra-kaku was a huge fan of Naseeruddin Shah's acting prowess. He singled out his performances in *Sparsh* and *Paar*. He was excited that Nandita was going to work with him. One day while on set, Nandita called Mr Shah and made him talk to Kaku. I observed all this from a distance. It was lovely seeing two of India's greatest actors speak so warmly about how they missed each other and how they would love to work together.

Kaku was unbelievably appreciative of the performances of his co-actors. Let me narrate one incident which I found quite remarkable. Soumitra-kaku had always told me how he thought Sabitri Chatterjee was one of the greatest actors Bengali cinema had seen over the years. One day, much after his shoot was over for the day, and we were supposed to continue shooting with Nandita Das and Sabitri Chatterjee, I saw him sitting in a corner silently. I went up to him and told him that his shoot was over and he could go home, lest my team had not communicated the information to him. He told me that he had stayed back to watch Sabitri Chatterjee perform. "Suman, it is still such a delight to watch her act. Just notice the comic timing in the scene she just shot," is what he said.

He was such a pleasure to have around in sets. His innumerable stories from yesteryears and anecdotes from his experiences as an actor were a treasure trove. Over my interactions with him for fifteen more years I found out that he possessed a fund of never-ending stories. For example, during the shooting of *Abhijan*, Robi Ghosh and he were casually chatting with each other and Kaku was narrating an incident which involved using the choicest cuss words. At one point, Robi Ghosh realized that Satyajit Ray had come up and was standing behind Kaku. Kaku did not realize this and continued in full flow. Suddenly he saw Robi Ghosh making strange facial expressions, trying to alert him. Kaku turned around, utterly embarrassed that Ray had been privy to everything he had said. Making light of Kaku's mortification, Ray remarked, "*Shono, ja bolbe censor bachiye bolo.*" (Listen, whatever you say keep in mind the censors.) They all burst out laughing.

Another time he told us that in his early years he had a problem shooting in the sun – he would find himself involuntarily squinting. The reflectors on set only made it worse. Ray suggested that he should avoid sunglasses in order to correct the problem. The eyes would then naturally adjust to the sun since the relevant eye muscles would be activated as a result. He diligently followed that for the rest of his life. Over the fifteen years that I interacted with him I never saw Kaku wearing sunglasses. Such stories were entertaining for sure but now I realize how much of an education it was for me and everyone else.

His performance in *Podokkhep* garnered him his first National Award. It is quite unbelievable that even after performing in many unforgettable roles throughout his career he had never received a National Award till 2006. Previously he had got a 'special mention' for his role in Goutam Ghose's *Dekha*, which he had refused. Astonishingly, the best actor award that year had gone to Anil Kapoor for the forgettable film, *Pukar*. For an actor of Soumitra-kaku's stature, delivering one of his finest performances in *Dekha*, it must have been humiliating to be relegated to a 'special mention' while a film like *Pukar* got the best actor.

That led to a prickly situation when his performance in *Podokkhep* came up for consideration. Many years later when I met him during a film festival, the film-maker Buddhadev Dasgupta let me in on a little secret. He was part of the jury the year *Podokkhep* was in the running. The jury was unanimous about giving the best actor award to Soumitra-kaku. However, since he had refused the 'special mention' for *Dekha*, they were not sure he would accept. So, Buddhadev Dasgupta left the deliberations and called Soumitra-kaku, telling him that the jury had decided on him, but would he accept? They did not want a situation where they picked him and he refused. Only when Soumitra-kaku expressed that he was willing to accept the award did they go ahead with the announcement.

Later I used to often jokingly tell him that though the award hardly meant anything to him given what he had achieved in his career, it set my film career going riding on his shoulders.

**The neurosurgeon in *Dwando* (2009)**

This shot from the shoot of my second film, *Dwando*, remains one of the most indelible memories of my professional relationship with Soumitra-kaku, providing a glimpse of his commitment to and understanding of the craft of film-making. A long trolley would charge at him while he would be moving within the camera frame. Now, the difficult part of the very long take would be that since the camera was charging forward, he would have to adjust the space within which he would be able to move as the shot progressed. The timing of his walk would need to be adjusted as the camera came closer to him. He was supposed to walk with a limp, holding a glass of scotch in his hand. He had to walk over the trolley rails not looking at them and hence there was every possibility of his tripping on them. Also, since his frame would become tighter as the shot progressed, he would be required to change his physical acting all along to adjust with the framing. To top it all, the extremely intense scene had very difficult dialogue using a lot of medical terminology.

Our cinematographer Barun Mukherjee was quite tense as it was a very complicated shot for him too. It was unlikely that we could go for another take if something went wrong – whether it was the focus, or the framing or a trolley jerk. Before the shot, Soumitra-kaku told me to check everything since he too wanted to do it at one go. I called out 'action' and what followed was a one-take shot almost four minutes long and impeccably performed. The entire unit started clapping in sheer joy, watching this legend enact yet another of his memorable scenes.

In *Dwando*, he plays the role of a neurosurgeon, an immensely successful doctor, but a solitary soul as far as his personal life is concerned. What I wanted to emphasize in the character was a neurosurgeon who considers his profession similar to that of an artist of the highest order. He finds beauty and solace in aspects of the medical profession that a standard person would abhor.

Soumitra-kaku's preparations as an actor had two primary stages which, using economics terminology, I would characterize as macro and micro. At the macro stage he was keen to understand what the director had in mind for the role. What I did with him was give him books related to the theme of the films – not necessarily about his role. For *Dwando*, I remember giving him *Proust Was a Neuroscientist* by Jonah Lehrer. Then we talked about doctor friends we both had. I knew a world-famous Bengali neurosurgeon based in the UK. I had already made plans for Soumitra-kaku to meet him.

I remember the dinner we had at Bengal Club when Dr R.P. Sengupta met Soumitra-kaku. It was indeed one of the finest conversations that I have been privy to. Here was one of the world's top neurosurgeons conversing with a world-renowned actor. I kept prodding Dr Sengupta with constant questions, coaxing him to talk about his personal life, his failures, and his insecurities and so on and so forth. He also spoke about the most challenging medical cases that he had tackled. I remember that after the dinner, when I was dropping Soumitra-kaku home, he told me, "Suman, this was perhaps the best input I could have for the role." The conversation gave him an insight into the mind of a neurosurgeon which he would imbibe in his portrayal. This was part of his macro preparation.

To digress a bit, I want to discuss an incident that gave me another insight into Soumitra-kaku's world-view. Dr R.P. Sengupta is the founder of the Institute of Neurosciences, Kolkata, a leading neuroscience centre. When we were shooting *Dwando*, the hospital was just about to begin operations and Dr Sengupta used to visit the shoot often to guide Soumitra-kaku with his inputs on the character. I remember that as the shoot came to a close, Dr Sengupta came forward with a 'letter of support' for the institute for Soumitra-kaku to sign – the standard fare like 'best wishes for the institute, etc.'. The letter ended with the words 'God Bless You'. Soumitra-kaku read through the letter and requested Dr Sengupta to delete the words 'God Bless You'. Clearly, he did not believe in God in that sense. His God was more Tagorean in concept.

*Nobel Chor*

Returning to the preparations for *Dwando*, after the meeting with Dr Sengupta, Soumitra-kaku started thinking about the micro aspects. He would ask me about his make-up, the costumes I wanted him to wear, his gait, and other specificities that I might have. I had told him that I wanted the doctor to walk with a limp – the reasons for which I wanted to keep opaque. I had a backstory for that (which would not be part of the film) and he could create his own backstory. The story I had in mind was that he had a defect at birth and that had scarred his mind for life. Maybe that is why he was bitter, and that would explain his cantankerous temper, as portrayed in the film. The reason I kept it opaque was that I wanted the audience to form its own backstory while retaining an element of intrigue about the character. We exchanged notes on that.

I had etched out his character very meticulously starting from his look and his attire. For some reason, I wanted a bald look with a French beard. I do not exactly remember why; maybe Pritish Nandy's look is what I had in mind. Given that Soumitra-kaku had so many engagements, in other films and theatre, he could not shave his head for the bald look but the rest we did. His character in the film, Dr Mukherjee, is a man of refined tastes – the kind who would have a scotch while listening to Western classical music every evening after work. Both of us discussed his attire. In the light of his Westernized outlook, we decided he would wear a suit at work and a house coat at home. He is dressed in the house coat in the last thirty minutes or so of the film. So it was crucial to get that right. I remember discussing the colour and texture of his coat. This was all decided keeping in mind the colour scheme of the sequence. Barun Mukherjee, the DOP, and I had decided to shoot that section in a sepia tone, and hence his coat had to be chosen accordingly.

I remember an interesting incident around the house coat. Our crew was all prepared to shoot the last scene at an old North Kolkata mansion – Dr Mukherjee's home in the film. It involved an intricate lighting job and Barun Mukherjee lit the house over two hours. After Soumitra-kaku came for the shoot (the call was in the evening since it was a night scene), he was intrigued by the nuanced lighting. He looked through the camera and complimented Barun-da on the lighting. I was worried that the house coat hadn't arrived yet. But when it arrived, I was shattered. It was nowhere close to the brief that I had given. I had no idea how to proceed. Here was Soumitra-kaku all ready for the shot, the lighting was done but I could not think of going ahead with the shoot with that house coat. It looked cheap and non-classy. The entire character would fall flat and with it the entire film.

I decided to tell Soumitra-kaku. I accepted blame for the fiasco. I should have checked the house coat much before. Somehow it had slipped my mind. I took the house coat to him. I asked him if it was okay to cancel the shoot that day. He understood and remarked, "*Hyan, eta toh jatra partyr coat.*" (Yes, it does look like a cheap coat they use in local jatras.) I apologized profusely but he went on to compliment me for taking the courageous decision to cancel the entire day's shoot, even though it implied a huge financial loss. The next day our costume designer found a coat from somewhere which was exactly what I was looking for.

Going back to his characterization – he was single, his wife had passed away years ago, and his work was his only passion. As mentioned before, the interesting aspect of his character that I wanted to bring out was that he considered his work as a surgeon akin to an artist. I have observed this trait among many well-known doctors. The intricate surgeries they perform are no less than a work of art, where the scalpel is like a brush and the canvas is the human body. Dr Mukherjee considers himself an artist of the highest order. What makes it even more significant is that human lives are at stake in his case. There is a dialogue exchange where Sudipta, the protagonist of the film played by Ananya Chatterjee, accuses him of lacking in the finer aspects of life – poetry, art, music, etc.

**Sudipta**

*Apni janen … oi apnader rokto mangsher bairey ekta jogot achey*? [You know, there's a world outside your world of flesh and blood?] Art, poetry, music … That has nothing to do with your … world of … machines actually, you treat the human body as a machine.

**Doctor**

Yes, absolutely … but a machine which bleeds. Important difference.

**Sudipta**

*Shekhaney beauty khujey paan apni*? [You find beauty in that?]

**Doctor**

Of course! *Ke bolechhey shekhaney art, beauty … sensitivity nei*? *Aaj ke* [Who says there's no art, beauty, sensitivity in that?] … just today I had a wonderful experience … *Bhabun toh … Ekti dosh bochhorer meye* … [Just imagine, a girl only ten years old] … she had a tumour in her cerebellar vermis. *Takey prothome boshano hoi … tar mathata shamner ekta frame er shongey … hyan, bolte paren bedhey rakha hoi … Tar mathata prothome kati … khub shabdhaney … kenona taar shira gulo harer khub kachh diye jachhilo … amar assistant rokto porishkar korey* … [You could say that first we bound her head to a frame … then cut open her head … very carefully because the nerves passed close to the bone … my assistant mopped up the blood] … what we call irrigation. And then, and then … finally it lay exposed, the tentorium – the tent … (NOW VERY SLOWLY HE SAYS THIS … ALMOST ROMANTICALLY) … a pale delicate structure of beauty, like the little whirl of a veiled dancer.

*Tar tolai cerebellum … jetake apnara gheelu bolen …* I allowed gravity to draw the cerebellum down … *taar por janen … taar por dekhtey pelam … tumour ta ekta laal rokto mangsho pakiye achhey … shetake ketey badh ditey …* [and then, you know, I could see the tumour wrapped in blood and flesh … to cut that off …]

(INTERRUPTED BY SUDIPTA)

ALL THIS TIME THE CAMERA OCCASIONALLY CUTS TO THE FACIAL EXPRESSION OF SUDIPTA … INITIALLY NONCHALANT BUT SOON TURNING TO DISGUST AS SHE CAN'T TAKE IT ANYMORE.

**Sudipta**

Stop it!

**Doctor**

A few millimeters here, a few millimeters there has potentially disastrous consequences. Imagine such cases … such interesting cases … *erokom dhorun diney du to, bochhor e kom korey holeo 250 ta* [say, around two a day, at least 250 cases in a year] … Isn't it fascinating?

**Sudipta**

Just stop it … right there.

THE DOCTOR IS CALMLY APPRECIATING THE WHISKY IN HIS GLASS.

**Doctor**

Medulla Oblongota, cerebellum … *Brain er ek ekta ongsho … kobitar shobdor moton mone hoina*? [Medulla Oblongota, cerebellum … parts of the brain … doesn't it sound like poetry?] … 'I am the poet of the body and I am the poet of the soul.' *Apni bodhoi janen na je* modern neuroscience is now discovering the anatomy underlying Whitman's poetry. *Ki bichitro na*? [Isn't that extraordinary?]

The way Soumitra-kaku managed the delicate balance between hurting his accuser and underlining the poetry in his job as a surgeon fascinated me and the crew. When I look back and think, I wonder how he did that. It was primarily the rhythm of his dialogue delivery and change in the intonation of his voice that did the trick. Of course, he had memorized the dialogues so well that he did not have to concentrate on remembering the difficult medical jargon, which I insisted he couldn't change even a single word of. Not an easy feat by any measure.

And, finally, justifying his action, he quotes from the Mahabharata. His dedication was such that in order to get the dialogues written in chaste Sanskrit right, he called up the great Mahabharata scholar Nrishinga Prasad Bhaduri from the shooting floor. He made sure of certain words and their pronunciations and then shot the scene. I believe that the variety and the complications he brought out in the character of Dr Mukherjee in *Dwando* was as exceptional as any other character in his remarkable oeuvre.

### *Peace Haven* (2016) and end-of-life questions

Five years later I was making my fifth film, *Peace Haven*. He was again my protagonist. But in the interim our relationship had deepened. From being 'The Soumitra Chatterjee' he had become my beloved 'Kaku', a father figure. Though during this period I made two films which did not feature him – *Shyamal Uncle Turns off the Lights* and *Kadambari* – I met him regularly and chatted with him as usual.

*Shyamal Uncle…* was my first experimental film, based on an experience my father's friend Shyamal-kaku had. It is about an eighty-year-old man obsessed about switching off street lights near his home which are on even after daybreak. The utter waste of government resources appalled him. Though others around him seem to be least bothered, the principles by which he led his life made it impossible for him to sit around doing nothing. Shyamal-kaku was a Marxist. He used to often lament the culture of malls in Kolkata and all the bright 'lights' when people were dying of hunger just a few miles away.

I remember telling Soumitra-kaku the story in one of our addas at Saturday Club and he immediately asked me who was playing Shyamal Uncle. I told him that Shyamal-kaku was playing himself in the film though he had no experience as a professional actor. Soumitra-kaku almost pleaded with me, wanting to play the role since he found the character fascinating. I explained to him that I was planning to make the film in a cinema-vérité style and with a non-professional cast. The reason I could not cast him in the titular role was that once he walked on the streets of North Kolkata (we shot the film in Sinthirmore and Paikpara), there would be hordes of people just to watch 'Soumitra Chatterjee' and that would ruin my vision for the film. He still insisted though, probably appreciating the logic of my argument, he said he would make himself 'invisible' and mingle seamlessly with the crowd as a common man. He, however, knew instinctively that his popularity – the fact that he was such a recognizable face – would not allow him to blend in inconspicuously and that would be detrimental to the film.

I decided not to cast him in the film. It went on to win awards and was programmed in major film festivals all over the world, including a special screening at the Museum of Modern Art (MOMA) in New York. Later, a number of people told me: Just imagine what you have lost – Soumitra Chatterjee doing the role would have made it even more memorable. In fact, one of my biggest regrets is that I could not release the film in Kolkata, not even in Nandan, since the then CEO told me that they could not screen a film which had only non-professional actors. I was told, "*At least serial korey, erokom cast nitey parten.*" (You could have at least taken actors who work in Bengali serials.) Soumitra-kaku in the main role would have made it so much easier but I am glad that I could stick to my vision. Though Soumitra-kaku would often chide me good-naturedly for not casting him as Shyamal Uncle, he applauded my integrity.

Coming to *Peace Haven*, I was in a bit of a dilemma. It was a film on 'death'. Normally Soumitra-kaku was quite nonchalant about 'death' and we talked about the matter quite objectively and with humour. He hated the sentimentality around death and treated it as an inevitable truth. In fact, later I realized that when I was writing the film (along with my co-writer, Arindam Ghosh) I even incorporated parts of our conversations and his views on the subject into the script. But ever since he was diagnosed with prostate cancer in 2010, for which he had to undergo treatment in England, he had become a bit sensitive about the topic. He would often tell me that he could 'see it' coming now. I had often complained to Kaku that he had become a bit less vivacious, as if crossing eighty had infused a fundamental change in him. Given this backdrop, I was initially uncomfortable about mentioning the film to him. Moreover, I wanted to mock death in my film – that's the philosophy I wanted his character to portray. That is how he used to think of death before being stricken by cancer.

To my surprise those things did not matter at all. His appetite for good work had not diminished an iota and that took precedence over everything else. I remember the excitement on his face when he heard the script for the first time. It was as if he had become the same man I had met ten years back during *Podokkhep*. He was all charged up.

What more could I ask for when Soumitra Chatterjee, at the age of eighty-one, called me the night before the shoot and discussed his costume, his dialogues and other nitty-gritty for the next day? For a rookie film-maker this was such a gift and inspiration. For a scene in *Peace Haven*, I needed the characters to climb a mountain so that I could shoot at the peak. During script-reading, when I asked him whether he was okay to get on a *palki*-type structure, which my team had made, he insisted that he would do the trek on foot. Incidentally we were shooting at the same location (Mama Bhagne Pahaar) where he had shot *Abhijan* over fifty years ago.

Given that all three protagonists were well into their seventies and eighties, I was also uncomfortable shooting at Keoratola crematorium or at the real mortuary near Park Street called 'Peace Haven'. I could sense that they were also a bit uneasy, though as thorough professionals they never let that come between them and the shoot. If anything, Soumitra-kaku, Arun-kaku (Arun Mukhopadhyay) and Paran-kaku (Paran Bandopadhyay) had a blast on the shoot. We would often wait for them to complete their adda for our shoot to begin. Apart from Kolkata, we shot in Boplur and Tajpur. I remember in Bolpur, the three of them used to call me to join their addas in the evenings after we were done with the shoot for the day. I knew that both Arun-kaku and Paran-kaku were wonderful singers but I heard Soumitra-kaku sing for the first time. He stunned us with his singing voice. Then all four of us sang in chorus – Tagore songs and even *tappas* of the great Ramkumar Chattopadhyay.

I cannot forget my experience of the last scene of the film where the three friends are at the beach sitting on a bench. The scene entailed Soumitra-kaku breaking down when his friend (Arun Mukhopadhyay) asks him rhetorically, "The last seventy-five years that we have lived … what does it add up to after all?" We were supposed to shoot the scene at 5:30 a.m. The entire unit was staying at a hotel in Tajpur where the scene was to be shot at the wonderfully quaint beach there. The previous night, at around 10 p.m., someone from the unit told me that Soumitra-kaku was calling me to his room. At first, I was a bit concerned given his health. I went to his room and saw that he was engrossed in his thoughts.

Typically, the day before shoot he had this habit of going over his scenes meticulously. When he saw me, he asked, "Why am I breaking down here?" He had an explanation himself but he wanted to know what I had in mind when I wrote it. The character was written pretty much keeping his actual persona in mind – a scientific mind who did not care much about death. I remember telling him, "Kaku, this man is like you. The character was written with you in mind. A rational, scientific mind, non-sentimental, a brilliant sense of humour, nonchalant about death, even mocking death. But I am not sure how you will react the day you face a situation like this – looking at death so to speak. This is just what I think will happen. But please don't tie yourself to what's written in the script. I just want you to think about your life in a flash. Your childhood in Krishnanagar, your parents, coming to Kolkata, Satyajit Ray, your life as an actor, your family … all of this will be gone when you die. Imagine the moment just before your death. You are facing the ocean, facing death. Think of your life … the past eighty years. Now you know this is it. The end. What do you want to say? Let the scene flow from there. Then let your emotions take over … or not."

There was a brief moment of silence. He looked at me and said, "Okay. Thank you." I left the room.

The next day we all saw what unfolded and which is now mentioned as one of the most poignant scenes involving Soumitra Chatterjee and death. I did not know what he would do. Tagore and Jibanananda were like his spiritual mentors. He chose a poem by Jibanananda to bring the scene to life. In a career that had innumerable memorable sequences, I think the final monologue in *Peace Haven* measures up to the very best. It is a rousing example of the kind of value addition he brought to a character, a sequence. I think the sequence has acquired a greater resonance now that he is no more.

Interestingly enough, this particular shoot was also the only occasion I remember Soumitra-kaku getting 'angry' with me, though given his professionalism he never demonstrated it openly. My production manager Saubhik reminded me of this. We had been shooting since 5.30 in the morning, which meant he had been up and about from 4.30 a.m. By the time we were lighting up for the last shot of the film, it was already dusk. For a while we saw him in the distance, engrossed in an adda with Arun-kaku and Paran-kaku, often asking my production people how much longer it would take and that he had been at it for over twelve hours. I was aware that he was feeling tired and hence losing patience. Then, suddenly, we saw him starting to walk towards us purposefully, visibly agitated. It was quite a long walk and we were actually supposed to pick him up in a car and bring him to the spot where the shot was being set up. My production team was a trifle unnerved. Given our relationship, he did not say anything to me directly, but told my production manager within my earshot, "*Boyesh ta monay rekho – 5.30 theke…*" (Please note my age – I have been here since 5:30.) Needless to say, I was embarrassed but helpless. Thankfully, we wrapped up the sequence quickly enough.

The way I looked at it, *Peace Haven* was a film that had to break genre conventions. It would start as a neo-realist film and then slowly approximate a cinematic equivalent of what is called 'hallucinatory realism' in literature, a genre pioneered by Chinese Nobel laureate Mo Yan. I wanted the three old men to experience life after their existence in the current world and that would be the ultimate exploration of death. Somehow the real and the unreal would unfold seamlessly throughout the film. The cinematic structure and the language of the film would also have to be in tandem with that narrative structure. Soumitra-kaku lauded my boldness of thought when he heard the script but warned me that it would be difficult to implement. But he was all for it. *Peace Haven* was one of Kaku's favourite films.

He was quite disheartened that it had scant viewership in the theatres when it released. I knew beforehand that given the strange structure of the film and the topic of 'death' as the main theme it would not have much of a chance at the box office. Nonetheless, we went ahead with the experimentation. The film was feted at a number of film festivals all over the world. It had its world premiere at the Busan International Film Festival and was selected at MAMI, Mumbai, and the New York Indian Film Festival in 2016. The film caught on later when Netflix acquired it and that delighted all of us.

"The film's innovative approach has to be lauded … starting off as a black comedy mocking death, and then seamlessly getting a surreal makeover. Something like this has never been attempted in Bengali cinema. Seen from the perspective of world cinema, this is a brilliant work. I hail it." – Soumitra Chatterjee on *Peace Haven*

## Nature and the human lifecycle in *Basu Poribar* (2018)

*Basu Poribar* is a Bengali adaptation of James Joyce's famous novella *The Dead* which is a part of his collection of stories *Dubliners*. I had been wanting to make this film for years, ever since I was in college. I remember reading the story and thinking how it would be apt for a Bengali adaptation. I was not even an aspiring film-maker at the time and so I thought how an Aparna Sen or a Rituparno Ghosh could do justice to the brilliant story. After that, while studying film at Cornell, I harboured the wish of doing it myself, if ever I could make films, that is. Little did I know that the rights of a Joyce story were well beyond the means of any Bengali producer. I left it at that and went ahead with other story ideas I had. Around 2015 I came to know that the rights of Joyce's works had expired and were now in the public domain. By then I had completed six Bengali films and was perhaps in a more comfortable position to take up this challenge.

Before I embarked on the project, it was imperative that Soumitra-kaku and Rina-di (Aparna Sen) agreed to be part of it since the entire story was based around the relationship of the two characters I wanted them to play. I could not think of any other actors. As usual in one of my addas with Soumitra-kaku I conveyed my desire to make the film. Joyce was one of his favourite authors in English literature and I could sense his excitement. I told him that I wanted to adapt the story to the Bengali milieu. I discussed with him how some of my favourite contemporary authors like Anne Enright, Tana French and Roddy Doyle were Irish. Of course, W.B. Yeats, who introduced Rabindranath Tagore to the West and was instrumental in his getting the Nobel Prize, was also Irish.

Soumitra-kaku said that apparently Tagore had written of the similarities of Bengali and Irish cultures, one of them being a sense of strong familial ties and gatherings around food.

The original setting of the Joyce novella was a family Christmas gathering which I wanted to change to the couple's fiftieth anniversary get-together. The story pivots around the relationship of the couple (though they were guests in Joyce's story) and hence making it their wedding anniversary would bring out the irony.

After the script was finalized, I narrated it to all my actors. By then the proposed film had taken on the dimensions of quite a multi-starrer. Apart from Soumitra Chatterjee and Aparna Sen, the film also had Rituparna Sengupta, Jishhu Sengupta, Saswata Chatterjee, Sudipta Chakraborty, Kaushik Sen – all big names in the Bengali film industry – apart from legendary actors like Lily Chakraborty, Arun Mukhopadhyay and Paran Bandopadhyay. In the first script-reading session my assistants playfully commented that it was almost a snapshot of Bengali cinema history. As with all the actors, I had prepared a very detailed backstory for Soumitra-kaku's character. Here is a very short synopsis of his character sketch.

**Pranabendu Basu**

> *Born in 1940, Mohishadol. Early education at the local school there. His family was the zamindar of the region. They had received the title of Rai Bahadur from the British. A brilliant student in school. Grew up with all the privileges and attitudes of a zamindar. Used to go hunting with his father and uncles. The family hosted well-known ustads on night-long musical soirees – his grandfather was a connoisseur of music. Went to Scottish Church College in Kolkata after school. Studied physics, then took up law. Went abroad in 1960 to study law. Returned in 1965 as barrister. Was a regular at Coffee House addas with friends at Scottish*

*Church. Keen interest in politics. Considered Churchill his guru. Admired Subhas Bose. Since Gandhi-ji had opposed Bose, was antagonistic about Gandhi. At a time when the Coffee House was abuzz with Jibanananda, Shakti Chattopadhyay, Samar Sen, Pranabendu's interest lay in politics. Never very keen on poetry and romanticism. But the veneer of sophistication he acquired thanks to his trip abroad hid that well. Never a huge fan of Rabindranath, but could recite a lot of his poems by heart.*

*Embarked on a successful career in Kolkata High Court. Met Manjari at the Coffee House. Took an instant liking to her but hesitated to say anything, primarily because of his ego. Serendipitously, their families brought about the marriage proposal. Though after marriage Manjari often said that Pranabendu had followed up on that with great passion. Of course, Pranabendu did not agree. When Manjari wanted to pursue a career after marriage, Pranabendu had no objections. They had a healthy relationship, were compatible, though Manjari never took to Pranabendu's patriarchal attitude. It was difficult to say whether that attitude owed itself to his zamindari lineage or was influenced by Churchill or Subhas Bose.*

My discussions with him were based around that. My main job at this stage was to enable him to get to the roots of the character and that's half the job done.

One interesting anecdote about this film pertains to the last narration – in essence the last two pages of James Joyce's *The Dead*. It captured the philosophy of the Joyce story and also our film. Given that it is one of the best written pieces in literature ever, I was having a chat with Soumitra-kaku on this. I told him that to summarize and translate the Joyce piece in Bengali was beyond my linguistic capabilities. I was planning to request my friend Srijato, a renowned poet and lyricist in Bengal, to do the translation. Soumitra-kaku very generously said, "Suman, can I try it? Please feel free to dump it if you don't like my attempt. You can ask Srijato then."

I didn't know how to react – a part of me told me that I had secretly wanted this. After a couple of days, he called me to his house and narrated what he had written. Then and there I knew that I had the perfect end to my film. He gifted his write-up to me ("*Darao … fair kore dichhi*," is what he said – wait, let me write it down properly for you). I have framed it and kept it as a prized possession. Here is the English translation of the same (though the Bengali one which he wrote was unique and not amenable to translation):

> The rains did come, after all.
> They say it has to rain on Ultarath.
> Did it rain as hard the night Sajal waited for Manjari outside her window?
> The call of death which drew Sajal … was it because of his unrequited love for Manjari?
> I don't know the answers…
> But this much I realize today … even as we lie trapped in our microcosm of suffering and grief … that has no effect on the rhythms of Nature.
> As if today an ancient curse rises from within this old behemoth … it haunts us … lashes out at us … reminds us … that out there in the vastness of this world, lives a bigger truth … it transcends the small world of suffering and grief we hold so dear…
> It took me fifty years of my marital life with Manjari … But I finally get it … for me, this is a cause for celebration…

> My fragile pride in my ancestry … the fading pride of a nebulous past … a river that flows no more … Even the crevices of my apparent success make me realize that there is a bigger truth, a bigger realization beyond all of this.
> I hear it in the incessant pitter-patter of the rain outside.

Shooting with the entire cast was an experience in itself. Initially I was quite apprehensive about managing such a huge cast, and that too such big stars. Almost the entire film was shot at the Mohishadol Rajbari near Haldia, a town around 100 kilometres from Kolkata. By then Soumitra-kaku had stopped going on outdoor shoots for his films since he was not keeping well. I was glad that he made an exception for my film. Deepa Kakima, his wife, told me, "*Tomar chhobi bolei jachhey.*" (He is going only because it's your film.) To my delight the entire cast was extremely cooperative with me throughout the process. It was lovely seeing the legendary pair of 'Soumitra Chatterjee and Aparna Sen' once again. Starting with Ray's *Samapti*, they had been together as a pair in so many other legendary films such as *Akash Kusum*, *Basanta Bilap*, *Baksho Badal*, *Chhutir Fadey*, to name a few. There was a beautiful warmth in their relationship. I loved to hear their conversations mainly around books that they had read and were planning to.

I remember a moment that will be etched in my memory forever. During a night shoot, a generator had malfunctioned and we lost power. Soumitra-kaku was preparing for the scene and going over his dialogues with the script. Seeing his frustration at the sudden unforeseen interruption, Rina-di immediately switched on her phone torch and told him, "*Tumi poro. Ami alo ta dhorchhi.*" (You read. I will hold the light.) I could not resist the beautiful moment and clicked a photo of them, I must admit without telling them. Later I did show it to both of them.

There were several occasions during the shoot when Soumitra-kaku helped me. I remember two such instances vividly. There was a scene towards the end of the film when Prahlad (played by Arun Mukhopadhyay) was supposed to leave the dining room. While doing so, it would strike him that when he had looked earlier, one of the lights in the chandelier was not working. He would stop and look back, and realize that he had been right – one of the lights indeed wasn't working. When he was acting it out, I found his look predetermined – it was not coming across as organic. I had two problems. One, I was unable to understand what exactly was going wrong. That is, why was I finding it 'predetermined'? And two, I did not know how to communicate that to such a legendary actor in front of the entire cast without offending him. I went up to Soumitra-kaku and told him my problem. He listened to me intently and then went up to Arun-kaku and whispered something to him. I do not know what he told him. But the next take was bang on. Arun-kaku in turn came up to Soumitra-kaku and thanked him.

In another scene, debutant Sreenanda Shankar was supposed to be with Soumitra-kaku. She was obviously nervous and told me so. I went up to Soumitra-kaku and told him, "Sreenanda is quite nervous about shooting with you in this scene. This is her first film and one of the first scenes that she is shooting. Can you do something about it?" Soon, I observed him going to Sreenanda and starting to chat with her. By the time the lighting was done and we were ready for the shot, she was much relaxed. The scene went quite smoothly.

The climactic dinner scene in the film gave me yet another glimpse of how great he was as an actor and his willingness to adhere to the director's vision. He was supposed to become emotional about his family while reciting Tagore. I was to take a close shot of him and hence the minutest facial gestures would be caught on camera. He performed wonderfully but I did not like the couple of teardrops that fell from his eyes. I applauded his performance, as everyone else did, but I went to him and told him that I wanted another take since I did not like the teardrops. He asked me, "Why? They came naturally." I told him my reasons. Pranabendu, his character, was too arrogant to cry in front of his family. Even if he did truly feel emotional, as he did then, he would hold back his tears. I wanted his eyes to be moist but without the teardrops. Soumitra-kaku understood and we shot again. This time it was perfect. He did the same rendition of the Tagore lines with his eyes moist but not a single teardrop. Such was his technical mastery over the craft.

The day *Basu Poribar* released he came for the premiere but was rather unwell. He could not stay for the screening. He ultimately saw the film a year later when I organized a special screening for him and Kakima at our studio. He was quite pleased with the film and looked at me and said, "*Khub ekta kharap korini … bolo*?" (I was not that bad … was I?) I just smiled and hugged him.

Who knew that this would be my last film with him.

> "What a pleasure it was to be part of *Basu Poribar*. The huge cast, so many characters … with different traits … all coming together to create a bittersweet experience. It keeps us spellbound right to its end which, though steeped in a haunting melancholy, is uplifting at the same time. That's what makes it so special. It's a film that's close to my heart." – Soumitra Chatterjee on *Basu Poribar*

**A guest role: *Nobel Chor* (2012)**

My first two films – *Podokkhep* and *Dwando* – had Soumitra-kaku as the protagonist. When I wrote *Nobel Chor*, I did not have him in mind for any of the characters. But my producer, Ashwani Sharma, wondered whether I could ask Soumitra-kaku to play the part of a 'mastermoshai' in the film. He was lured by the idea of having two of India's greatest actors, Mithun Chakraborty (who was already cast as the protagonist) and Soumitra Chatterjee,

*Peace Haven*

in the film. I was elated by the suggestion too since my association with Soumitra-kaku would continue, though he would have a guest role. Soumitra-kaku also readily agreed to act in the film. It was only a few days of shoot with him in Bolpur and a day in a village near Kolkata but it was nonetheless fun to observe his dynamics with Mithun-da.

He was playing the role of a village schoolteacher. As usual, his preparations for even a guest role were top notch. The first thing he wanted to perfect was the Bolpur accent. I need to mention here that he had an amazing ability to master different Bengali accents from different parts of the state. In the process, I noticed one thing that really touched me and is a lesson for all actors. Soumitra-kaku had mastered the accent but in his first scene with Mithun-da he noticed that Mithun-da was not being able to speak in that dialect. Instead, he was speaking in a normal dialect with certain words enunciated in a way to convey a rustic feel. Amazingly enough, Soumitra-kaku sacrificed his authenticity and started speaking the way Mithun-da was.

As far as actors' dynamics go, this needs to be emphasized. Usually, I have observed that there is a subtle tussle among actors on sets. Oftentimes it is healthy, namely, it is good for the scene and the film, but all too often it becomes unproductive. Each one tries to outdo the other which ultimately harms the scene. And here was a perfect illustration of how Soumitra-kaku gave way to his co-actor in order not to outshine Mithun-da in their scenes together.

Another day involving a shoot in village near Kolkata is memorable for a different reason. Mithun-da and Soumitra-kaku were part of the sequence. It was Mithun-da's last day of shoot. He was supposed to leave for Mumbai the next day and his dates were not available for months after that. There were predictions of rain and the sky was overcast. By the time we reached the location, the weather had worsened. We would have at most an hour or so in which to complete an entire scene. I had made my shot divisions carefully but given the immense pressure, I could not figure out how to complete such a scene in an hour.

Mithun-da and Soumitra-kaku took over. They saw my shot divisions and restructured them so as to economize on the time it would take to shoot without sacrificing the detailing of the shots that I had planned. Basically, that would entail them breaking their acting rhythm and shoot in order to minimize time. The last part of the scene, which had its acting arc at one level, would be shot right after the establishing shot, and then the interim shots would be canned. In a few instances, the reactions would be shot first and the other actor would act out as per the reaction of his partner. Usually, it's the other way round. And those were very specific reactions, not random cutaways. I understood how difficult it would be for them, but I knew I was working with two of the best in the profession. It also needed extreme understanding and cooperation amongst the actors, not to mention mastery over their craft.

What unfolded was pure magic. This is the scene where Bhanu (Mithun-da's character) comes to Mastermoshai with the Nobel medal, not knowing what it is. Mastermoshai explains its significance to him and the fact that it was stolen the day before from Santiniketan. It was a pivotal scene and both of them performed with unbelievable fluidity. The general chaos with the approaching rain and the time pressures did not seem to affect their performance at all.

During shoot I was privy to many conversations both of them engaged in. Mithun-da used to remind Soumitra-kaku how he loitered around sets just to observe the likes of Uttam Kumar and Soumitra Chatterjee when he was an aspiring actor. They used to talk about their days of working with Mrinal Sen, Shakti Samanta and other greats, replete with anecdotes and lessons on cinema. I loved this story from Mithun-da's repertoire while shooting Mrinal Sen's *Mrigaya*. It was Mithun-da's first film and that too with a master and hence he was all pumped up. I had once asked Mithun-da how he was so perfect in his choreography with lights while acting. It is as if he knows, subconsciously, when to take the lights the DOP wants him to take and when to leave the lights for his co-actors.

Apparently, *Mrigaya*, which was shot by the legendary K.K. Mahajan, had a scene that had been precisely choreographed beforehand by Mrinal Sen and Mahajan. When the scene was being shot, Mithun-da poured his heart into it, in the process forgetting about his spots which had been preassigned according to Mahajan's lighting. Mahajan was on top of the crane when Sen called 'cut', realizing that though the performance was brilliant, he could not keep it since Mithun-da was off mark. Mithun-da did not understand why a 'cut' had been called. Mahajan climbed down the crane and slapped Mithun-da in front of the entire cast and crew. Hurling the choicest expletives, he told Mithun-da, "What do you think we were doing for so long? Wasting our time?" Mithun-da never forgot that slap. Never again in his career would he miss his mark.

Uttam Kumar taught him another lesson. He had acted in a Bengali film called *Kalankini Kankabati* (with Sharmila Tagore), which Uttam Kumar directed. One day while shooting a close-up, he called Mithun-da. "*Ei Mithun, edike ai. Tui to lokkhi tera. Amar moton. Shon, konodin directly camera lens er dike takabi na. Chhoy inchi pashey takabi.*" (Hey, Mithun, come here. You have a slight squint. Like me. Don't ever look at the camera lens directly during close-ups. Look six inches away.) That was a suggestion Mithun-da followed his entire life. Somehow nobody had told him that he was *lokkhi tera* before. Soumitra-kaku in turn narrated incidents about Uttam Kumar which fascinated Mithun-da.

Thank god, my producer had insisted on casting Soumitra-kaku for the guest role. I would not have had such experiences with two of my favourite actors otherwise.

# Interlude

## The Child (in) Soumitra Chatterjee

Around four years ago, Deepa-kakima (Deepa Chatterjee) and Soumitra-kaku wanted to see my daughters, Maya (four years old at the time) and Leela (two years). Once they reached Soumitra-kaku's place they promptly realized that they would have to entertain themselves. They had some sort of fantasy land in mind, which apparently required ransacking the elegantly decorated living room. My wife and I were extremely embarrassed, but the person who indulged them the most was Soumitra-kaku himself. His only worry was that their house was not suitably child proof. Maya and Leela were pleasantly surprised to get a playmate ... maybe seventy-five years older than them. But did that matter?

Then again when Soumitra-kaku received the Legion of Honour from the French government I called to congratulate him. Maya wanted to talk to him too. This was the conversation which followed:

Maya: Did you win a prize?
Soumitra Kaku: Yes, some sort.
Maya: I want too.
Soumitra Kaku: Sure, but you will get bigger prizes when you grow up.

*This assurance probably satisfied her.*

*Their last interaction with Soumitra-kaku was during the lockdown in June 2020. They watched Sonar Kella and were fascinated. They sent a video message for their friend Feluda, which Poulomi-di showed to Soumitra-kaku. Kaku was hugely excited to get a new fan of Feluda at the age of eighty-five. He sent a very sweet 'Thank You' back to them.*

*During the last couple of years Kaku often expressed the desire to spend a few days with Maya and Leela in Santiniketan. I was not comfortable with the idea since he was not keeping well but I was on the verge of relenting if he so strongly wished.*

*My first film Podokkhep is the story of an old man (played by Soumitra-kaku) and his relationship with a five-year-old child. It represents the cycle of life where at the end a human being becomes like a child, going back to the womb in a sense. Soumitra-kaku was like that in real life, quite literally so. He was an eighty-five-year-old child. I am reminded of that whenever I think of his relationship with Maya and Leela. I am waiting for them to grow up and see Apur Sansar, Charulata and the rest. One day they will realize who their 'friend' was.*

# 4

# A Soumitra-kaku Adda Session

**Soumitra-kaku** (*on the phone*): Listen, Suman … what are you doing tomorrow evening?

**Me**: Nothing much. Shall I come over?

**Soumitra-kaku**: Can you? We can chat.

**Me**: Sure. What time?

**Soumitra-kaku**: Seven? Is that good?

**Me**: Sure. I will be there.

*Ever since I met him, these adda sessions were what I used to wait for eagerly. Either at his house or at Saturday Club. So exactly at 7 p.m. I would be there at his bungalow in Golf Green. Given how particular he was about punctuality I made sure that I was present there at least fifteen minutes ahead of time. At 7, I was inside his house, waiting in his exquisitely decorated living room. He used to come down from his room upstairs soon after. On his shoulders he had his 'jhola' which had all the paraphernalia he needed – his medicines and his very precious diary where he maintained his dates. By now it is well known that he did not have a manager and kept a note of all his dates and schedules himself. As soon as he saw me, he used to flash his wonderful smile and say, "Eshe gechho?"* (*You are here…*) *Apart from my parents he was the one person whose blessings I sought by touching his feet. Let me relive one of those cherished addas, one we had after I had returned from the US after a long time.*

**Soumitra-kaku**: You returned from the US two day's back – correct?

**Me**: Yes. This Thursday.

**Soumitra-kaku**: You must be jetlagged?

**Me**: Got used to it.

**Soumitra-kaku**: How is Vidhi (*my wife*) and the kids?

**Me**: They are fine. They will come in the winter.

**Soumitra-kaku**: Let's plan our Santiniketan trip then. We have to do it this time.

*He had often expressed his wish to spend a few days with my daughters, Maya and Leela (who were four and two years old respectively at the time), in Santiniketan.*

**Me**: Yes, if your health permits.

**Soumitra-kaku**: Health permitting or not. We must. (*Laughs*) Talking of health, let me get our drinks. Scotch is good?

**Me**: Sure.

**Soumitra-kaku**: Have you tried Blue Label by the way?

**Me**: No … it's so expensive. I wonder whether it's worth it.

**Soumitra-kaku**: Let's find out. Someone presented this to me. Give me a minute.

*He is gone for exactly a minute and back with a bottle and two glasses.*
*He asks the house help to bring ice.*

**Me**: Let me pour it.

**Soumitra-kaku**: Okay. Please…

*I pour us our drinks. We do 'cheers' and resume our adda.*

**Me**: Did I tell you? I went to Istanbul recently. For an economics conference.

**Soumitra-kaku**: O really?

**Me**: Such a vivacious place.

**Soumitra-kaku**: Did you hear the bells? Which Orhan Pamuk mentions in his book on Istanbul?

**Me**: You remember?

**Soumitra-kaku**: Of course. Thanks to the book I feel I have already visited Istanbul. How vividly he describes the city. What a writer … Hopefully someday I can go to Istanbul. By the way, how is your research going?

**Me**: Good, good … I am working on a new paper on corporate social responsibility.

**Soumitra-kaku**: Can you elaborate a bit? As much as I can understand, that is…

**Me**: Sure, it's not quite rocket science. So basically corporates are concerned only about profits, so I am working with a co-author on how to make corporations care about improvements in society too along with making profits. Situations where both can be achieved in tandem.

**Soumitra-kaku**: Quite interesting … what happened to your previous paper? On microlending … you had mentioned Grameen Bank.

**Me**: Oh, that got published in a very reputed journal, *Journal of Development Economics.*

**Soumitra-kaku**: That's good to know. Congratulations!

**Me**: Thank you, Kaku. Amazing that you follow up on my research ... apart from my scripts. (*I laugh*) Any interesting films that you have done recently or are supposed to?

**Soumitra-kaku**: O yes, Atanu (*Ghosh*) is doing a film called *Mayurakshi* which I am really excited about. It has Bumba (*Prosenjit Chatterjee*) too. He is playing my son. I really liked the script.

**Me**: That's wonderful. And what about your theatre projects?

**Soumitra-kaku**: I am doing a small part in Poulomi's play. Apart from that I am translating Ibsen's *Ghosts*. I want to stage it. Oh, did I tell you I loved *The Vegetarian*? (The Vegetarian *is a Booker Prize-winning novel by the South Korean author Han Kang.*)

**Me**: No, so you got that?

**Soumitra-kaku**: Yes, yes. Actually, Rina (*Aparna Sen*) presented it to me. Apparently, you had suggested that to her.

**Me**: Yes, I recommend it to everyone. It is a book of rare brilliance.

**Soumitra-kaku**: Absolutely, genre bending. It takes you into the strange mind of the protagonist in a very interesting way.

**Me**: By the way, I brought some books for you.

*The books were by the Chinese Nobel Laureate Mo Yan, a book by Knut Hamsun, one by Jhumpa Lahiri and another by Zadie Smith. His eyes light up in delight.*

**Soumitra-kaku**: Thank you so much. I have to hide them from your Kakima since once she takes them, they end up someplace in the house I can't find. (*Laughs*)

**Me**: But the Jhumpa Lahiri book is for Kakima.

**Soumitra-kaku**: That's fine. Let me read it first and then I will give it to her. Don't worry.

**Me**: Mo Yan is simply fascinating, the way he writes satire is like no one else I have read in recent times.

*He browses through the books hungrily. His phone, an old model of Nokia which hardly anyone uses, rings. He says he is quite a Luddite and hence this is good enough for him, he does not need a smartphone. I don't think I have ever seen him text.*

**Soumitra-kaku** (*on the phone*): Yes, speaking. O yes … when is the event again? Okay, please hold on. Let me check my diary.

*He opens his dilapidated diary which has all his dates – his film shoots, his theatre rehearsals, the many events he has to attend and other family engagements.*

**Soumitra-kaku** (*on the phone*): Yes, tenth looks fine. It was already blocked for you.

*He disconnects the phone and turns to me.*

**Soumitra-kaku**: This is the Kolkata literary festival. They are organizing a session with me and Sharmila (*Tagore*). Should be interesting.

**Me**: On Satyajit Ray?

**Soumitra-kaku**: Yes. I believe so. It would be nice to meet Sharmila again. Haven't met her in ages. I have wonderful memories of her and Tiger.

**Me**: Like?

**Soumitra-kaku**: Oh … many, many. I remember one time Tiger and Sharmila were staying at the Grand. We drank till 4 in the morning. The next day I was supposed to shoot for my song which became such a cult, "*Khirki theke shingho duar*", and he had a Ranji trophy match at Eden. We were both worried as to how we would manage after this rendezvous. Surprisingly, next day I was very happy with the song picturization and Tiger scored a century. Those were the days. (*Laughs*)

**Me**: What did you all talk about?

**Soumitra Kaku**: Anything under the sun. Cricket, politics, or travels … cinema. Did I tell you the Collie Smith story? I think Tiger told me about it.

**Me**: No, please go on.

**Soumitra-kaku**: So, Collie Smith was a Jamaican-born West Indies Test cricketer. He used to play with Sobers. People used to say that Collie Smith was in fact more talented than Sobers. So, the story is that the team was in London … I think it would be late 1950s or early '60s. Sobers was driving the car and both of them were going for a charity match when the car hit a truck. Smith was in coma for three days. After he was declared dead, his body was flown to Jamaica where over 50,000 people gathered to pay their last respects to the future of West Indian cricket. Imagine Sobers's guilt. He did not know how to face Smith's mother. So apparently Sobers went to her and told her, "Mama, I cannot bring back your son but I promise that whenever I play for our country from now on, I will play for me and for Collie." This was early in his career and the rest is the stuff of legend. Sobers went on to become one the greatest in the history of cricket. Isn't the story fascinating?

**Me**: Absolutely. It is so poignant.

**Soumitra-kaku**: Brings tears to one's eyes. Sorry … I am just blabbering.

**Me**: That's fine. I love listening to you blabber. (*I laugh*)

**Soumitra-kaku**: How is your Hindi film coming along?

*I was writing my Hindi film* Aadhar, *produced by Drishyam Films, at the time.*

**Me**: It is at the writing stage now.

**Soumitra-kaku**: I so loved the concept. Wish you get to work with Irrfan or Nawaz … you know, I recently watched … what's the name? See, this is happening these days – I am forgetting names…

**Me**: *The Lunchbox*?

**Soumitra-kaku**: Yes, yes. What a brilliant film.

**Me**: It is. I am so glad that you got to watch it.

**Soumitra-kaku**: And both Irrfan and Nawazuddin are so good. I even called Irrfan after watching the movie.

**Me**: Really?

**Soumitra-kaku**: Yes, I got his number from someone … he was so elated to receive my call. I told him that I was jealous of his acting skills. He was mighty embarrassed. But you know, Suman … I really mean it. His acting talent is in the category of the greats – Balraj Sahni, Naseer, Shabana. Just see his nuances. I so loved him always but seeing *Lunchbox* I was simply bowled over. Even Nawazuddin. What a talent! By the way, what do you think of the drink?

**Me**: It is definitely very good. I have not had anything like this before. But I hold on to my initial view. It is not worth 200 dollars or something…

**Soumitra-kaku**: I also think so.

**Me**: By the way, this is your last drink. Remember that your doctor said that you are restricted to two?

**Soumitra-kaku**: You see, the doctor has officially said two drinks, but he also knows that it will get extended to three. So, he has been conservative in his count knowing this. And hence the third one is legit. (*Laughs*)

**Me**: Ha ha ha…

*I pour a couple of drinks for both of us. His security guard comes and tells him that the dhobi has arrived with the clothes. He asks him to let the dhobi in. The dhobi counts the number of clothes and tells him that the total amount is 170 rupees. Soumitra-kaku asks him to wait. Looks for his wallet. Takes out two hundred-rupee notes. The dhobi has no change but tells him that he will adjust that with the next round of clothes. He leaves.*

**Soumitra-kaku**: Did I tell you about my drinking sessions with Uttam-da?

**Me**: Really? Where was this? Where could two such superstars have a quiet drink without being mobbed?

**Soumitra-kaku**: Great Eastern Hotel. We had a place which was secluded. We used to decide that after shoot we would get together for our drinks.

**Me**: Interesting, since you probably know that for Bengalis it is a matter of eternal debate and it is assumed that there was a rivalry between the two of you.

**Soumitra-kaku**: Good rivalry. What you would call 'healthy competition'. He loved me like his brother and I respected him immensely. What an actor and so serious about his craft. You know, in the early days of his career he used to have a lisp due to which his pronunciation was compromised. And you know how he corrected it?

**Me**: How?

**Soumitra-kaku**: He used to get up early in the morning and read the 'panchali' (*Bengali verses in praise of deities).*

**Me**: That's amazing.

**Soumitra-kaku**: Isn't it? To read the panchali correctly one needs to use the tongue effectively. So, in a sense it was a wonderful exercise for his diction. That's how he corrected it. And remember he was already a star then. He probably need not have to…

**Me**: That's really astonishing. So, who would you say is the greatest Bengali film actor?

**Soumitra-kaku**: Tulsi Chakraborty. Without a doubt. He was a genius. God gifted. Just think about his performances … *Pather Panchali* of course, *Parash Pathar*, *Sharey Chuattor* … and so many other remarkable ones. Unfortunately, he lived and died in extreme penury.

**Me**: Yes, I have heard.

**Soumitra-kaku**: That's the scenario of Bengali actors. Such a great talent and … Oh and Sabitri Chatterjee.

**Me**: What did you think about Suchitra Sen?

**Soumitra-kaku**: Very beautiful lady and her charisma on screen was unparalleled. But I would never rate her as a good actor. Sorry.

**Me**: Achha, Kaku, in your lifetime you have interacted with people of such quality, not only in films but in the literary world too. Your friendship with Shakti Chattopadhyay and Sunil Ganguly is so well known. Given the cultural scenario in Bengal now, don't you feel a void?

**Soumitra-kaku**: I think it was Bernard Shaw who said, "If you trip in the darkness, shall you blame the dark?"

*His phone rings.*

**Soumitra-kaku** (*On the phone*): Yes, who is this? Please call me tomorrow morning. I can't talk now. Yes, I will see what can be done. Tomorrow morning.

**Me**: Kaku, I always wanted to ask you. When you look back … what are the events that you think impacted you at a very early age?

**Soumitra-kaku**: You mean when I was a kid?

**Me**: Yes, in Krishnanagar. You were born at a very interesting time. No?

**Soumitra-kaku** (*Thinks a bit*): One is surely the death of Rabindranath.

**Me**: But you were too young then – you remember that?

**Soumitra-kaku**: I did not know who he was. But I remember that our school declared a holiday. My brother returned from school, saying that the poet Rabindranath Tagore had died. I saw my mother holding the railing of our verandah and crying. That impacted me significantly. Just think about it, a poet has died and a housewife is in tears because of that. I immediately thought – wow, who is this man? I vividly remember that image – my mother crying.

**Me**: Indeed, it's poignant.

**Soumitra-kaku**: And that quest is still on. I have never lived without Tagore ever since. I remember another thing which impacted me tremendously. The famines took place around that time. I remember so many people out in the streets. They used to come outside our house pleading, "*Ektu maar debe, Maa*?" Uff! – that anguished cry. Just imagine, they wanted some 'maar' to survive. Not even rice. My mother used to give them rice. Whatever we could afford. (*Maar is gruel – basically the froth/starch extracted from rice when cooking.)*

**Me**: Interesting that years later you acted in one of the most significant films based on that famine.

**Soumitra-kaku**: Yes, life is so interesting. I think that experience helped me with my character in *Ashani Sanket.*

**Me**: Amartya-da has written about his experience about the Bengal famine quite poignantly.

**Soumitra-kaku**: Of course, and one of his most important work is *Poverty and Famines*, no?

**Me**: Yes. Very important indeed.

**Soumitra-kaku**: How is he by the way? What a mind … Did I tell you, I met him at Nabanita-di's place? After all these years.

**Me**: Yes, you told me.

**Soumitra-kaku**: Recently somewhere it was remarked that 'Soumitra Chatterjee is the greatest living Bengali'. The stupid things people say. How can you even think that? Particularly when a mind like Amartya-da is there.

*Just then their house help comes and tells Kaku that Kakima was calling him. She is upstairs in the bedroom.*

**Soumitra-kaku**: Suman … just one minute.

**Me**: Sure, I think it is time for me to leave too.

**Soumitra-kaku**: Are you in a hurry?

**Me**: No, actually unless I go, my mother will not have her dinner. She waits for me.

**Soumitra-kaku**: I understand. Have one last drink then. I shall be back in a minute. Let me check what Kakima is saying. She is not well.

**Me**: Please.

*As Soumitra-kaku goes upstairs I check my unanswered calls and messages. I never kept my phone on while chatting with him. He comes back soon.*

**Soumitra-kaku**: Listen, Kakima told me to ask you, when can you come for lunch? She is feeling bad that she could not meet you.

**Me**: I will. Don't worry.

*After a brief pause, I raise an uncomfortable question which I wanted to ask him.*

**Me**: Kaku, I want to ask you something I always wanted to but I am not sure whether I…

**Soumitra-kaku**: Please don't hesitate. You know there is no formality in our relationship. You are family to me.

**Me**: Okay, talking about family … do you think that you have neglected your family in your life? Of course, you became an acting legend and such a big star but at times talking with Kakima gives me that impression. You know she has many grudges against you. I am asking this since I really feel for her and I dare say that I am closer to her than to you.

**Soumitra-kaku**: I understand. One thing is for sure – she has been my biggest inspiration. She has been my biggest critic as I have always told you. You see, Suman, my son and my daughter have been my ultimate love in life. I was a busy actor and I could not do many things with them which a normal father would do. But I have always made them my priority. I have also given them so much that a normal father would not do. You are close to both Mithil and Bubu. You can ask them. And as far as Kakima, yes … given that I have been a hero in films, and I believe I am moderately attractive, there have been romantic involvements, but your Kakima also imagines more than what actually happened. (*Laughs*) … by the way, did you pour our last drink?

**Me**: Kaku, this is going to be your fourth then. Aren't you crossing…?

**Soumitra-kaku**: Just half. One for the road as they say. I am meeting you after months, hence…

**Me**: Well…

**Soumitra-kaku**: This is officially cheating on my doctor. (*Laughs*)

*I pour two small drinks. After we finish, I tell him that I have to leave. He always insisted on coming outside and bidding me goodbye. He walks me to the gate. I get into my car and leave … cherishing all that we talked about for the last couple of hours.*

# Interlude

## The Painter

A few years back, when I went to Soumitra-kaku's house for an adda session he asked me whether I had some time to see something. Of course, I did, but I remember wondering what he wanted me to see. He went to a cupboard where many files and scrap papers were stuffed. From amongst them he took out a few sketches and paintings. I looked at him with a quizzical gesture - when he mentioned that these were his paintings. I had no idea that he used to draw. What astounded me was the sheer quality of the drawings and paintings. Many were just scribbles with a pen, many were charcoal drawings and many were full-blown paintings. He was shy like a child when I commented that I really thought they were brilliant. He told me that over the last few years paintings gave him solace as a means of expression. Subsequently, his paintings were publicized and I even attended one of his exhibitions which was inaugurated by Jogen Chowdhury in Kolkata. But what I am going to narrate now is an incident which truly brings forth the 'solace' aspect of his paintings.

In 2017, Soumitra-kaku's grandson, Rono, was involved in a near-fatal accident. I was in Miami and hearing about it saddened me immensely. First of all, Rono was a terrific budding actor who had just started his career. Secondly, I could not fathom how Poulomi-di, Soumitra-kaku and Kakima would cope with what happened. A couple of months later I went to India. Honestly, I did not know how to face Soumitra-kaku. When I went to his home the security guard at the gate told me that Soumitra-kaku was in his study. I went up to his *study and saw him splashing paint on a canvas. It was as if he was in his own world. He could not see me. I just stood there in silence and soaked in the moment. I could sense a strange kind of solace in his activity. It was almost after ten minutes, when he turned back to take something from the desk behind him, that he noticed me. "O ho, when did you come? Why didn't you wake me up?" I distinctly remember that he used the word 'wake'. Did the word emerge inadvertently ... perhaps not. Though I coaxed him to continue with the painting, he somehow felt guilty that I would be waiting for him. It was a strange figure that he was painting. Was it a self-portrait? I wondered. It was still unfinished, but I could see how it was his own way of handling grief. It reminded me of Tagore for some reason.*

# 5

# A Close Encounter with Death

It was probably around twelve years back. I do not remember the exact year. There was a small report in the *Anandabazar Patrika* that Soumitra Chatterjee had been admitted to the hospital for some heart issues, that he was well now and was supposed to be discharged the next day. I had read the article while in Miami and was relieved that it was only a minor health scare. Since I would be travelling to Kolkata next month, I did not feel it was necessary to call him.

The following month when I went to Kolkata and met him at his residence, I casually asked him about the incident. What I heard from him was rather shocking.

"Oh," he said, "I was almost going to die. You won't believe what happened."

His response piqued my curiosity.

He narrated the incident to me. He was alone in the house. Kolkata had witnessed torrential rain earlier that evening. Suddenly he experienced pain in the chest. He did not take it seriously but it kept getting worse. He realized that he was having a heart attack. All the usual signs were there. He started looking for Sorbitrate. In that state he climbed to his bedroom on the second floor. However, the medicine was not there in its usual place. By then he had called the hospital and asked for an ambulance. It was on its way but stuck in the waterlogged streets because of the rain. He kept on calling but there was little they could do at that point. Then he started looking for Sorbitrate everywhere. The situation was quite grave. Losing all hope and having severe breathing problems and chest pain he somehow decided to check the kitchen. Never in his wildest imagination would he have searched the kitchen for Sorbitrate, but it was perhaps his last desperate attempt. To his utmost surprise he saw the bottle lying there. Next to the gas oven. He immediately took the medicine and after a while his condition improved.

The ambulance arrived after almost an hour. He was taken to the nursing home and was kept under observation. The next day all the newspapers carried this news, albeit in a small column. The world did not know what had actually happened.

He laughed at the prospect of how Sorbitrate in the kitchen saved his life. Honestly, I was a bit shaken. The outside world had no idea that it had literally been touch and go for him – and that he owed his life to the fortunate discovery of 'Sorbitrate in the kitchen'.

I asked him, "What did you think of during that period? When you were almost sure that this is indeed the end?"

He replied, laughing, "Nothing but the Sorbitrate really. I remember thinking about your Kakima, Mithil and Bubu … that they would not know what exactly happened."

After that we had our usual adda and I came back.

Ever since, I kept pondering about the many discussions Soumitra-kaku and I had about 'death'. He used to tell me often that he could now see 'death' approaching. This was primarily after he was diagnosed with prostate cancer in 2010. His only wish was that it should come quickly, whenever it had to. He shuddered to think of himself as a burden to his family, suffering a slow and agonizing end. We would also talk about 'death' in literature and how authors have written about this phenomena – from Tagore to Tolstoy to Simone De Beauvoir. I always felt that Soumitra-kaku was quite cavalier about death. It was the ultimate truth and one should gracefully accept it – that was his viewpoint. It is interesting that later, in my film *Peace Haven*, I explored 'death' head-on, with Soumitra-kaku performing one of his most poignant acts on facing death.

After I returned from India, the incident kept haunting me. Such an icon, such a career, such a life and it was almost all over in a second – but for him chancing upon Sorbitrate in the most unusual of places. That led me to the question: "What if?" What exactly would have gone through his mind in those moments? In cinematic flashes maybe? His childhood in Krishnanagar, his theatre days, coming to Kolkata, Satyajit Ray, his family … what exactly would he have felt just before the final adieu to life? That chain of thought led me to wonder whether he could act out his death.

In his seminal work, *An Actor Prepares*, Constantin Stanislavsky had dwelled on questions of truth in acting. Wasn't this the ultimate truth? Thinking along these lines led me to an experimental cinematic idea. What if he had not found the Sorbitrate? What would it be like to have him act out his 'death' and I shoot his 'acting' of death? Whatever he thought in cinematic flashes I could shoot later, whether it was his family, or Krishnanagar, or whatever. Those montages would be interspersed with his acting of death and succumbing to the heart attack. So, basically, we would re-enact that entire evening, with the only difference being that he would die.

We can imagine the impact of the death of an icon and the subsequent drama surrounding his death. News channels competing to make the best capsule of his life, newspapers rushing to get obituaries from people close to him. BBC and *New York Times* coming out with obituaries. The world of cinema paying its respects to one of its finest ever. I would try to stage all this, as much as possible. I would shoot that and keep it for later use.

What came to my mind next was a bit controversial and rather morbid. What if we shoot his actual death? It wouldn't be possible if he passed away suddenly. In that case, we would have to shoot after his death. But if he was in the hospital, breathing his last, I could shoot him. Of course, I would need permission from his family. The real-life incidents that would happen after his demise would be shot as documentary footage. The final film would be an edited rendering of the two versions – Soumitra-kaku 'acting' his death and his actual dying. Wouldn't it be the greatest 'act' of an actor? How much closer to truth could one get? He would not even be alive to see whether his act was good or not. Is that even important? So many questions could be explored through this experiment.

I shared the idea with some close friends and family. The reactions were quite diverse. Only a few appreciated the bizarre experiment, but the majority was uncomfortable to the point of getting angry with me. "How can you think of exploiting the death of such an icon?" "How can you be so cruel to even think of such an idea?" Not that I did not expect such extreme reactions. That in turn left me wondering – were they right about that? Was I thinking of exploiting the death of my beloved Soumitra-kaku? Many such confusing questions hovered in my mind. Even if I knew that my intention was novel and purely artistic, would the world believe it? I grappled with such issues.

After a few years, I decided to tell Soumitra-kaku about my idea and the ethical concerns I was having. After all he was my closest friend, my philosopher and guide in life. Who else could I go to? Though this very sensitive issue concerned him, he was the only person who could analyse the situation with objectivity. With a lot of apprehension, I decided to broach the topic with him. I told him that I was going to say something to him which might have a permanent repercussion on our friendship. I could sense his curiosity. I told him about my idea and what made me think about it. The title of the film, if he agreed, would be *An Actor Prepares*. A take on perhaps the greatest book on acting written by Stanislavski.

I waited with bated breath. After patiently hearing what I had in mind, his first reaction was, "What a brilliant idea!"

Ever since we often talked about this bizarre project of ours. I got busy with my other films and so did he. But this was a secret project we very much wanted to do. Somehow it did not materialize.

During his last days in hospital, I was in constant touch with his daughter Poulomi. She sent me a photo of Kaku lying senseless. He seemed to be in a different world altogether. I wish he was acting, and I could tell him after the shot, "Brilliant, Kaku." He would turn back and ask, "*Theek chhilo*?" (Was it fine?)

Would it be too sentimental to admit that I have tears in my eyes even while writing this? Soumitra-kaku was life personified. That is how I will remember him – forever.

# Interlude

## Look Who's Come for Lunch

My parents are not star-struck people. Even though I interact with a lot of stars because of my involvement with the film industry, they have never expressed their desire to meet any of the stars I have worked with. The only exception was Soumitra-kaku. One day my mother asked me whether it would be possible to request Soumitra Chatterjee to come to our house. Of course she qualified her request by saying that if I thought it was not proper or that a person of that stature would not come to our house and that in turn it will be an embarrassment for me, she would understand. I was very touched with her wish and told her that I would definitely ask him.

When I asked Soumitra-kaku he told me effusively, "Of course, I will. Just tell me the date." After figuring out a date according to his schedule it was decided that he would come to our home for lunch. I went to pick him up from his Golf Green house.

In the meantime our home got a facelift, with the best bedcover out and the choicest curtains adorning our windows. My mother could not sleep the previous night. She kept thinking about the Soumitra Chatterjee movies she had seen since her childhood, starting all the way from Apur Sansar, Samapti, Charulata, Jhinder Bondi ... as if her life was unfolding in front of her eyes through the works of the legend. She could not believe that the very same actor would actually come to her home. She, along with our cook Archana-di, started cooking since morning. What will be the menu? Where will he sit on the table? Who will serve? Does he have diabetes since an elaborate sweet dish was being prepared? I smiled to myself and let her drown in her excitement.

When I came to the house with Soumitra-kaku they were delighted. I was impressed that within minutes Soumitra-kaku made all our family members so comfortable. He of course realized that everyone was a bit alert after he walked in, but he was just himself. He started talking about mundane things and the nitty-gritties of daily life which had nothing to do with his world of films and stardom. The beauty of all this was that he was not consciously doing that or putting up a façade. The conversation flowed smoothly and soon I found my parents and others talking to him like he was one of us.

The lunch was a pure Bengali - rather Bangal (East Bengal) - affair. My mother was elated to know that Soumitra-kaku loved 'muittha' - a Bangal delicacy made with Chitol fish which she had prepared with a lot of care. Soumitra-kaku really enjoyed the meal and I was so happy to see the joy on my mother's face.

After lunch we all chatted for some time and I arranged for a photo session with all of us and Kaku. Before leaving he thanked my parents for a wonderful afternoon. While returning home with me in the car it was interesting that he remarked, "Tomader puro poribar ke ki apon laglo. Ekta odbhut shohoj shorol byapar achhey." (I felt so close to your family. There is a simplicity about them which is so endearing.)

Aparna Sen and Soumitra Chatterjee in a still from *Basu Poribar*.

The cast of *Basu Poribar*. By the time the script was ready, the film had acquired the dimensions of a multi-starrer. As one of my assistants playfully commented, it was almost a snapshot of Bengali cinema history.

Two masters at work on location, *Nobel Chor*. As rain threatened to wash away the day's shoot, Soumitra-kaku and Mithun-da took over, restructuring my shot divisions so as to economize on time. It was an awe-inspiring demonstration of their mastery over the craft of acting as also cooperation between actors.

Nandita Das and Soumitra-kaku in a key scene in *Podokkhep*, the film that fetched him his first National Award for Best Actor.

A still from *Podokkhep*, which explored the relationship between a seventy-year-old retiree and a five-year-old girl.

The three musketeers in *Peace Haven*, Soumitra-kaku, Paran Bandopadhyay and Arun Mukhopadhyay. It's on location that we discovered what a wonderful singer Soumitra-kaku was.

Arguably one of the greatest scenes enacted by Soumitra-kaku, in a career teeming with glittering sequences. His rendition of Jibanananda Das infused the ending of *Peace Haven* with a rare pathos, lifting it well beyond what I had visualized.

FOOTSTEPS
a film by Suman Ghosh
A friendship, a bond, a rediscovery of life.
Starring
Soumitra Chatterjee
Nandita Das
WINNER Best Actor, Best Bengali Film Indian National Award '08
OFFICIAL SELECTION Vancouver International Film Festival '06
OFFICIAL SELECTION Karlovy Vary Film Festival '07
A legendary Indian actor in the performance of a lifetime.

SOUMITRA CHATTERJEE
PORAN BANDOPDHYAY
ARUN MUKHOPADHYAY
RANDOM WALK FILMS PRESENT
Official Selection
OFFICIAL SELECTION New York Indian Film Festival 2016
Official Selection MAMI
Peace Haven

দ্বন্দ্ব
Dwando
The Conflict
A Film By Suman Ghosh

VIGNESH FILMS PRODUCTION
THE BOSE FAMILY
A film by Suman Ghosh
OFFICIAL SELECTION Washington, DC International Film Festival 2019
OFFICIAL SELECTION New York Indian Film Festival 2019

# 6

# 'Happiness Is Like an Oasis…': An Interview[3]

Over the years, as I interacted with Soumitra-kaku, I realized that his thoughts and views on many facets of life should be preserved for posterity. Alas, the interviews I read of him, which were mainly for the promotion of a soon-to-be released film, failed to capture that. One might say that as a result of a mild frustration I decided to don the journalist's hat. I interviewed him on two occasions over the years, once in 2012 and then in 2018, which were published on his birthdays in those years. *The Telegraph* gladly indulged me in this new avatar and I am indebted to them. These interviews talk about his views on literature, politics, memories, his early life and also importantly on the craft of acting. A lot of the questions that I asked him pertained to topics I had discussed with him in our adda sessions but which I thought should be made available to the public. There is a lot to learn from them. Hence I am glad that through this book I got an opportunity to share the interviews with the readers.

---

3 This was originally published in *The Telegraph*, on Soumitra Chatterjee's birthday, 19 January 2012.

**Suman Ghosh (SG)**: Kaku, how old are you going to turn on 19 January?

**Soumitra Chatterjee (SC)**: Oh, that I don't know! But I know my birth year … 1935.

**SG**: So, how do you approach ageing?

**SC**: Frankly, the feeling of having to depend on someone else is a bit difficult to deal with. I'm scared of dependency. I have never really been dependent on someone till now.

**SG**: Looking back, would you consider yourself 'happy'?

**SC**: It's difficult to say that. Happiness in life is … temporary. It is like an oasis, if it wasn't present, life would be like walking in a desert. But talking about work, sometimes I wonder how much I can actually give to society through the work I do … Just a moment of happiness.

**SG**: I have noticed a change in your attitude towards life in the last two years. Your usual vivacious self is absent. Why is that?

**SC**: I would call it melancholia, because I am worried about how long I can continue working. I can feel the various constrictions that age brings and I'm growing increasingly wary about my life and work.

**SG**: Do you think you have been able to do justice to the role of a father and a husband?

**SC**: I think I have tried to, definitely. See, like so many other fathers and husbands, I have not been able to go to the market every morning, but I have tried to create a balance between work and family. Maintaining the balance is very important, otherwise happiness doesn't seep in.

**SG**: You have spent your life with stalwarts like Sisir Bhaduri, Satyajit Ray, Uttam Kumar … the list is endless. Do you feel a vacuum now that almost no one from your generation is there any more? How do you cope with the changing times and people?

**SC**: You know there is a quote by Bernard Shaw which goes something like 'if you trip in the darkness do you blame the dark?' It's true that my generation is getting wiped out slowly and I feel lonely thinking about the same. There is a vacuum. Probably because I am an escapist I can deal with the changes easily. I can't attend funerals and just don't think about the people around me passing away. Instead I keep myself busy with my work, with theatre and films.

**SG**: So how does Soumitra Chatterjee the actor prepare for a character-centric role? You can give an example of a film and explain…

**SC**: Okay, so let me tell you about *Sansar Seemantey*, which was written by Premendra Mitra and directed by Tarun Majumdar. For this film I had to extensively work out the look and traits of a thief. First, I thought about how the man would look and dress. I sat with the scriptwriter and director to decide the particular way his hair and face should be and the clothes he should wear. Even the make-up was decided. Next, the behaviour of the character was worked upon. His traits and the way he would talk or react to a particular incident. I read a few books for that to know how a thief might behave. In real life, no matter how much I might have seen people catch thieves or seen thieves trying to steal something, playing the role of a thief was a completely different experience. The process of building the character inside me was crucial. It had to be convincing. So there had to be an internal preparation and an external one.

**SG**: There has always been talk of the rivalry between you and Uttam Kumar. What do you have to say about that?

**SC**: See, rivalry is natural when you are in the same industry and you do the same work. But there was never a tense situation between the two of us. When I was in college, I remember, the Uttam-Suchitra pair was already a hit. While my friends admired Suchitra Sen and her capabilities as an actress, I was an Uttam Kumar admirer. I was doing theatre back then. Later on when I started working in films, I got to know him well. But I never really idolized him. I have idolized Balraj Sahni. I still believe he is the best actor our country has produced. Naseer (Naseeruddin Shah), of course, comes close.

**SG**: What was your relationship with Uttam Kumar like?

**SC**: It was very good. In fact, after our shoots, we used to go for addas at the Great Eastern Hotel. We used to chat till late. Let me give you an example of our relationship. Once, during a film shoot, he was getting stuck on a word and wasn't being able to pronounce it properly. There were a lot of takes and still he wasn't able to deliver the line. I was there and asked him what was going wrong. Mind you, we shared a very good rapport. He said after some time, 'Do something, go out for some time.' So I did. Then in one take he delivered the line.

When he came out, I asked him why he had asked me to leave and whether he was feeling uncomfortable in my presence. He told me, 'I was getting self-conscious. You have very clear pronunciation and I don't really have that.' He used to read the *Chandipath* and panchali out loud to improve his pronunciation. Remember, he was at his peak then. So a man who can talk about his shortcomings so openly and then overcome the same, deserves all the appreciation.

**SG**: Among recent Bengali films, has any performance stood out?

**SC**: I don't really get to see a lot of films nowadays, but I have seen some. Earlier I used to drive out and go watch films when I wanted to. Now because I can't drive, I don't get to watch much. In *Autograph*, Bumba (Prosenjit) was very good. I liked the fact that the character was very well defined and not overdone. I also liked *Moner Manush* but I think the dialect could have been worked on a bit more. Indraneil (Sengupta) did a very good job in *Angshumaner Chhobi*.

**SG**: And what about the actresses?

**SC**: Hmm … I think in *Saanjhbatir Rupkathara,* Indrani (Haldar) was very good.

**SG**: What is your message to the young actors of today?

**SC**: You know, somehow I feel many of them concentrate more on self-exhibition and less on their work. I would only tell them to concentrate on their approach towards work. Charles Chaplin is remembered today not for a particular incident that he was associated with or a single film. When his name comes up there are so many images that cross your mind. From him being a factory worker to playing Hitler and so many more such scenes. I think he is a great source of inspiration for actors across generations.

**SG**: Now the question without which this chat will be incomplete: what has been Tagore's role in your life? You had told me how you got to know about him when you were very young…

**SC**: I remember when I was in Class I, we were in Krishnanagar and on baishey srabon I didn't go to school because I wasn't feeling well. My brother who was two years elder to me came back from school very early, and when my mother asked him what had happened he said the school had declared a holiday because Rabindranath Tagore had passed away. My mother caught hold of the wall next to her and slid down, crying. That was my first impression of Rabindranath Tagore. A poet's death could bring tears to a housewife. I am sure this was true all over Bengal. That was significant for me.

Later in life, my father, who was a very good elocutionist, used to recite many of Rabindranath's poems to us while on his weekend stay at Krishnanagar (he had to be at the Kolkata High Court five days a week). I started reading a lot of his works, and was amazed at his capabilities as a writer. I'm not saying this because I'm a Bengali, but the kind of grasp he had over the language I don't think anyone else in the world did or does. His works influenced lives of so many people across society.

Hc has been a guide for me all my life. Whenever I am conflicted about something, I turn to Rabindranath the human being, not the writer or poet or artist. I wonder what he might have done, if he was in doubt about the same thing. I wanted to, rather want to, understand the man; he has been a fascinating influence in my life.

**SG**: What do you think about the large-scale celebration of his 150th birth anniversary?

**SC**: Of course there is a hujug (hype) associated with it and a business angle. But I think, to a certain extent, more and more people are getting to know about his work and appreciating it. The younger generation is getting to hear a lot of his songs from so many different sources and becoming aware of him and his work. In that sense it's good.

**SG**: You think people today are really imbibing Rabindranath Tagore?

**SC**: When my son recited Rabindranath's poems in school, I thought to myself, his works are being taught even now, and when I saw my grandson reciting one of his poems, I was glad that he and his works are still around us and that he lives within us.

**SG**: Let's move on to a different topic, politics. You are basically a Marxist. Given how the left transformed itself in places like China and Brazil, where they are still very much in power, what do you think happened with the left in West Bengal?

**SC**: Yes, I have been a leftist throughout, but that doesn't mean that I approve of the way that it works here in West Bengal. Things could have been done differently, maybe. When I read the *Communist Manifesto*, I thought the words held truth and in fact they do even today … When I was in college I went through this rebellious phase, probably like everyone else. I came close to politics during that time in my life.

**SG**: I have known you closely for more than ten years now. Only on one aspect did I not like your reaction or views … after the Nandigram incident. I think you said, "*Ja korechhey besh korechhey…*" (They did what was right.)

SC: No, you got it wrong. I had said '*chhaley baley koushole*' (by hook or by crook). I never said that for the wrong actions that were taken. Why will I say something like that? I said '*chhaley baley koushole*' when cadres were entering (Nandigram).

**SG**: That means you approve of violence to curb violence? Where is your Rabindranath?

**SC**: See, it isn't like that, violence is necessary in cases. You should definitely fight for what is rightfully yours. But other than that, I really didn't appreciate the way the matter was handled.

**SG**: What drives Soumitra Chatterjee? When you get up in the morning what do you look forward to?

**SC**: My work; I feel incomplete without work. I really don't know what I would do if I didn't get to work. It is a driving force behind almost everything else that I do. But you know, previously it was dreams with which I woke up, now it's *ashampurno swapno* (unfulfilled dreams).

**SG**: What would your last wish in life be, if you were told that would be granted?

**SC**: I don't know really … (*pauses*) I think, to pass away with dignity and peacefully.

# 7

# 'An Artist's Duty…': An Interview[4]

'I was born on 19 January 1935' – that's how he begins the conversation when I ask him his age. He completes eighty-three years today. He belongs to the class of Bengali intellectuals like Ravi Shankar, Satyajit Ray and Amartya Sen who, apart from making an international impact through their work, might rightly be called the last of the Renaissance Men.

Last year has been the most traumatic year of his life with Rono's (his grandson) accident. At the same time, professionally he starred in one of the biggest commercial successes in Bengali films (*Posto*), while his performance as a patient of dementia in the film *Mayurakshi* was lauded by critics all over the country.

When I asked him about how he keeps on performing like this when his mind is drained after such a traumatic incident, he replied, "Mind is not drained – it is blocked, there are barriers. And we need to remind ourselves that these barriers hide a flood of performances,

4 This was originally published in *The Telegraph*, on Soumitra Chatterjee's birthday, 19 January 2018.

creative aspirations, and emphasize the need to thrive through our acting. And at times like these, we need to overcome the barriers and open the floodgates for the performances to flow like a deluge, a waterfall."

This is Soumitra Chatterjee. The man with whom I have had the privilege of working in five films. He soon became a father figure to me and is now my best friend. Here he opens up in a freewheeling chat about his initiation into acting, about his craft and other aspects of life.

**Suman Ghosh (SG)**: Over the years, in more than sixty years of acting experience you have perhaps achieved everything and done so many different kind of roles. Looking back, are you satisfied as an actor? Knowing you, I know the answer is 'no' but nonetheless I want to ask you. What is it that you look for still?

**Soumitra Chatterjee (SC)**: Well! Not that I know clearly what I am looking for but I have a feeling within me that so many things have not been done and I could have done so many other things. I don't know what the other things are but I somehow feel that. May be the lack of good writing and content in Bengali cinema, which is pretty hackneyed, precludes me for exploring so many other roles. But sometimes even within such confines you come across one good story which is compelling, which is true and genuine, which in turn energizes me and kindles my interest in acting itself. That unfortunately happens to many good actors. I have never experienced this kind of apathy for acting anytime in my career but I must admit that sometimes I am on the verge of such a feeling.

**SG**: You are talking about lack of good writing and content in Bengali cinema but if you compare it with Hindi films, they have much better cinema coming out, not only now but over the years. In that respect I want to ask you that you got offers from many established directors in Mumbai – Hrishikesh Mukherjee offered you *Anand*, Shashi Kapoor offered you *Junoon* … you refused them. Do you regret not taking up those offers since you could have explored much more?

**SC**: No, not really. You see, even if I tried out in Hindi cinema there's no guarantee that I could be successful. Let me elaborate. There is some kind of chemistry that clicks in one kind of cinema and does not in another. I am sure I would have clicked mostly in dramatic and family stories but not in all kinds of films. I was not of that mettle. And the second reason is that when you work in the film industry of a particular place you have to embrace the culture. There I would have been a failure. And not only a failure, I would not have been satisfied. I always wanted to be an inner-directed man. I wanted to be what my inner self wanted to be. My soul would not have been happy outside Bengal. If I would have been a successful film actor in Mumbai, I would not have got time to pursue my other interests, say, in theatre.

**SG**: Let me go back to your formative years. Do you remember what made you choose this career in the first place?

**SC**: You know, I was attracted to histrionics from a very early age. It ran in the family. None of them were professional actors but some of them, particular my father and grandfather, had acting talent. They used to take part in amateur dramas. My father used to recite poems very well. We used to stage children's plays in the courtyard of our ancestral house in Krishnanagar. Mattresses were brought out for the stage, bedsheets were used for the curtains, and from the foil in the cigarette packets my parents made crowns for us to be used in the plays. And then as soon as I started going to school, I found another opportunity to act. I used to take part in plays that were staged just before the winter holidays or during Saraswati Puja. I started receiving prizes for these. Let me tell you a funny incident. Those days after a play some members of the audience would declare prizes by shouting, "I declare a medal for so and so…" Even if the person making the announcement did not have a medal to give away at the time, since it had been declared he would make sure to deliver a medal to my house. I started getting them so often, it turned out to be one of the main reasons I became an actor. That was the initial spur. Those medals were so attractive for me. I was a very ordinary student in the school. I never used to read books prescribed but I was extremely attracted to books outside my curriculum. Thank God for that.

**SG**: What kinds of books did you read?

**SC**: All kinds of books. I read *The Resurrection of Tolstoy* when I was thirteen or fourteen years old.

**SG**: Was there a culture of books in your family?

**SC**: Oh yes. Very much. In our house there was a small room where we had almirahs stacked with books. When we were growing up, my parents used to constantly buy books. Though we were not in a good shape financially, they never compromised on books. I still remember my parents reading Tarashankar's *Hashuli Baaker Upokatha* and discussing it. I got exposed to those discussions. And at that time I was a very naughty child. I was almost uncontrollable – breaking things, hitting other kids and everything else you can think about. My parents were fed up with me but they knew how to calm me – by giving a book to read. Like Pavlov's dog, books used to make me forget everything else. My sister was married to Ramaprasad Mukherjee, son of Ashutosh Mukherjee. He had a huge library – he was famous for his voracious reading – which had all kinds of books from mathematics, to travelogues, on Sanskrit to everything else in the world. As children we used to go and play in the library amidst those books. That left a huge impression on me.

Apart from books I remember watching movies in Krishnanagar. My parents did not support me seeing movies at that age. So, I had to bunk classes and see those surreptitiously. I was also caught doing so sometimes. In a small town everyone knew everyone and someone used to go and complain to my parents that they saw me in the theatre. Let me tell you a funny incident. My parents had gone to see a film which was not for children. Of course, I saw that on my own. When my parents were discussing a particular scene I intruded into their discussion and burst out saying, "Why that other scene was also…", thus giving away my secret. Thinking back, I realized that those initial years of watching Hollywood movies in Krishnanagar got into my subconscious mind and probably influenced the fact that I became a movie actor.

**SG**: How do you prepare for a role? If you could illustrate, citing a famous role you have essayed?

**SC**: My first film, *Apur Sansar*, might be quite instructive. Of course, Satyajit Ray had thought of me for the role in *Aparajito* but found me too grown up at the time. Afterwards, when he went to Venice for *Aparajito* where it got the Golden Lion, he declared that he would make the third part of the trilogy. When he came back from Venice, he sent for me. When I went to his house, he asked me whether I was still interested in acting and whether I still went to Sisir Bhaduri for theatre. I never realized that he was making me talk all the time since he was interested in finding out how good I was with the language. He was very particular about that. He just mentioned that he was going to make the third part of the trilogy and might need me. He never mentioned that it was for the main role. He asked me to read the novel once more.

Then he asked me to visit his shoot one day. He was shooting *Parash Pathar* and I remember it was the day he was shooting for the party scene. All the famous Bengali actors were there in the scene and it boosted my confidence.

Then I went for his *Jalsaghar* shooting. One day after the shoot got over, while I was leaving, he took me to Chhabi Biswas. He introduced me to the great actor and it was then that he said that I would do the main role in *Apur Sansar*. It was the first time I had heard that. I could not believe what had just happened. I was ecstatic. I remember that the shoot was taking place in Aurora Studio in Maniktala. I took a bus from there to Dalhousie, where I was working as a radio announcer. I will never forget that bus ride. I wanted it to go faster, keeping pace with my excitement.

**SG**: By the way, I think many people don't know that before your job as a radio announcer you were a LIC (Life Insurance Corporation) agent and you were a complete failure in that.

**SC** (*Laughs*): Yes, in one whole year I could get just one client and that too was my own elder brother. I could not convince anyone else in one whole year.

**SG**: So, after that day what was the next thing Ray asked you to do for your role as Apu?

**SC**: He gave me a draft of the script. After a few days he gave me a brief resume of Apu's character. And I on my own started preparing certain things about Apu's character from the script itself. You see, in a standard screenplay there is a time lapse between scenes. So, I started asking what Apu was doing in the interim period. I started writing a diary of Apu and from that bringing out the characteristics of the character. I took it to Satyajit Ray. I thought he would laugh at me. But he encouraged me a lot. I remember him saying, "Soumitra, you have written here in the diary that Apu went to his friend's hostel and spent time discussing literature. But how about if they went to watch a film instead?" He was provoking me with questions and egging me on. Unfortunately, I have lost those notes of his and my diary.

**SG**: And what else did you do with him as preparation?

**SC**: Of course, there was a general preparation. During that time, I had a distaste for cinema. I was more into theatre. I was very snooty and had the typical snobbery of a theatre actor that it is a superior platform as an actor. But after watching *Pather Panchali* I was totally bowled over. I never imagined that something like this could come out of Bengal. After being selected as Apu that was my benchmark of film acting. Satyajit Ray took me with him on Sunday mornings to watch Hollywood movies that used to come to Kolkata. That was a grooming for me.

**SG**: Do you remember which films you watched with him?

**SC**: Yes. We saw *The Lost Weekend* by Billy Wilder. He pointed me towards what to watch out for in the performance of Ray Milland. According to him, Ray Milland was the last word in film acting. After the show, he asked me what exactly I liked about the acting. That was the education for me.

**SG**: I want to ask you about the character in *Abhijan* since it was diametrically opposite to your normal self of a Bengali bhadralok. How did you prepare for that?

**SC**: I can tell you that I have gone through all things 'obhodro' too. At one point of my life when I lived in Howrah, I used to spend a lot of time with bus and taxi drivers. So, the body language, the dialect and the language came from my experience of those days. By the way, do you know that *Abhijan* was not supposed to be directed by Ray? He was just expected to be the scriptwriter. But then all of us coaxed him to direct. I am grateful to him that he agreed to change the language in the script with inputs from me since I told him that I have experience living with such people.

**SG**: I was enthralled by your performance in the just released Bengali film *Mayurakshi* where you play a patient of dementia. How did you prepare for that?

**SC**: I had enough of preparation on this before … much before *Mayurakshi*. Many years back I made a telefilm called *Asamapto* which was also directed by Atanu. So around that time I had read many books on Alzheimer's patients. And around then my uncle was diagnosed with Alzheimer's. After that my elder brother was diagnosed with dementia. So, I had lots of reference points but also one should have a viewpoint to empathize. That is absolutely crucial. Only information through books is not enough. You should have a mind such that the patient's sufferings should bring tears to your eyes.

**SG**: It seems that you bring aspects from your vast experiences and readings in life to the forefront when you need to play a particular role. What people call emotional memory…

**SC**: You know, in one of my first writings on cinema acting (in a journal edited by Satyajit Ray) I had given an example from my growing-up years. During the summer, when water levels in the river were low, villagers kept their boats immersed in water until the levels rose in the post-summer months. The boats had to be kept under water so that they would not 'dry out' and remain ready for the seasonal operations. This analogy holds true for actors as well. I think we should all keep absorbing all the experiences and anecdotes around us all the time – even when we are waiting for the acting 'season' to open up. We need to remain absorbed, with our thoughts and expressions, all the time, and use this latent learning when the next suitable role comes up. This is the essence of my philosophy – like the boat in the summer time, I keep myself immersed, learning from people and events around me all the time.

**SG**: Talking about two forms of acting in theatre and cinema – and since you have been active in both throughout your career – do you think they are complementary? Many famous actors like Naseeruddin Shah and yourselves have done this but at the same time many haven't.

**SC**: I would describe the two as sister art forms. They are not very different from each other. You can always recall your experiences from each other. Often when I am doing theatre, I decide that here I will use my film acting craft and vice versa.

**SG**: You have repeatedly told me how you are so impressed by the acting talents of Irrfan Khan, Nawazuddin or Manoj Bajpayee in current Indian cinema. What is it that you find so admirable?

**SC**: Brevity. The essential aspect of an actor's weapon is brevity. With so little effort they express so many things. This is true not only of this current lot but also of other great actors like Naseer or Om Puri. This comes from training and thought.

**SG**: Can you give an example of brevity in a performance that readers can identify with?

**SC**: Let me take the example of one of the greatest actors on the Indian silver screen and my idol, Balraj Sahni. When you see him as a cobbler in *Garam Hawa*, just observe the way he enacts that. Such simplicity in how he works on a shoe … it is as if he is doing nothing. He is exerting so little. Similarly, when he climbs down from the tonga in the last scene, does he do it with aplomb? No, not at all. He does it because his political faith and his social appreciation of Indian history have given him such sensibilities that allow him to behave like a common man believing in this.

**SG**: You have lived your life amidst such people, not only in films but generally. There has been a cultural degradation for sure in Bengal. We have talked about this. How do you overcome this suffocation? I always see the vivacious self of you amidst all this.

**SC**: Because I love art in general … but that's rather vague. My sustenance comes from literature. You find me vibrant today morning because I wrote a poem last night. It is not poetry of the highest level but that does not matter. It is very important for me personally. By loving literature, I have loved the essence of art.

**SG**: Let me end this with a poignant question. The last year has been so tough on you personally given your grandson's accident. How do you maintain poise in the face of such a tough time personally and still deliver memorable roles even now? I particularly know this since I shot with you last year right after that incident. The role you enacted was that of a flamboyant zamindar. How do you mentally do that at a time your mind is so drained?

**SC**: The mind is never drained. It may be blocked. It is the artist's duty is to open the blockade and bring out the waterfall.

# Interlude

## The Night of the National Awards

It was the 54th National Awards in 2008. My debut film, Podokkhep, starring Soumitra-kaku, received two awards. One for the best Bengali film and the other major one, the first-ever best actor award for Soumitra Chatterjee. The ceremony was attended by the film glitterati from all over India. It was fitting that Tapan Sinha got the Dadasaheb Phalke Award that year, posthumously. That year, Vishal Bhardwaj and his team received multiple awards for Omkara, Vidhu Vinod Chopra and his team for Munnabhai and Dibakar Banerjee's wonderful debut film Khosla ka Ghosla got awarded, among many others.

But the star of the evening was clearly Soumitra Chatterjee. When he went up to receive his award there was a standing ovation from the entire film fraternity. It was such a pleasing sight, especially for me, when they showed clippings from Podokkhep on the screen up there. Soumitra-kaku was the main attraction in the after-ceremony events. We could not even go near him.

Back in our hotel, I got a call from Soumitra-kaku at around 10 p.m. He asked me, "What are you doing?" I told him that I was preparing to retire for the night. Then he suggested that if it was okay with me why didn't I come to his room and sleep there? Apparently there were two large beds in his suite and we could have a nice chat too. I went to his room immediately. It was only then that I got to know the real reason from him. He had *vertigo and his room was on the top floor of the hotel. Given his health he preferred someone to be with him. I found it quite endearing that he had requested me to come to his room and stay with him. After chatting a bit I switched off the lights and then our 'adda' continued for quite some time. We talked about Kolkata football, about Bibhuti Bhushan's novels, about the recent India-Pakistan series and so much more. After a while he fell asleep.*

*I kept thinking about the man sleeping next to me. Earlier in the evening, I had witnessed his stature in the eyes of the world, the thunderous applause still reverberating in my ears. The great thespian, Feluda ... but what struck me was that none of this had any effect on him. He was more worried about whether Sourav Ganguly could continue after the Greg Chappell saga, what had gone wrong with Kolkata football and sundry other things. All the adulation, his stature, his image, hardly had any impact on him.*

*So far in our association, he had been Soumitra Chatterjee to me. It was only my first film with him. But that night he became my Soumitra-kaku. Not the legendary actor but a father figure, whose impact in my life for the next fifteen years or so would be so profound.*

# 8

# An Equal Music[5]

## Amartya Sen and Soumitra Chatterjee

During the question-answer session following the screening of my documentary film, *The Argumentative Indian*, at the Nandan auditorium one afternoon in 2018, Soumitra Chatterjee was seated to my left and Amartya Sen to my right. It was a massive gathering of people from the media and the intelligentsia. Before the function commenced, I felt it necessary to clarify a certain point. Soumitra Chatterjee is two years younger than Amartya Sen. Yet, I address him as Kaku (uncle) and Amartya Sen as Da (short for Dada, elder brother).

This is an academic tradition – this addressing of senior Bengali academicians as Da, be he a Nobel laureate or even forty years senior to one. Unless this is clarified, one may consider it an audacity on the part of the speaker.

5 This was originally published in Bengali in *Anandabazar Patrika on* 17 March 2021. Translated for this edition by S.K. Ray Chaudhuri.

Interestingly, immediately after this, Amartya-da took the microphone and said, "Following the Santiniketan tradition, this Da may even mean Dadamashai [grandpa]." The audience burst out in applause and laughter at this humorous response from him. I felt it necessary to refer to this before writing the piece lest I am deemed audacious or impudent.

I consider myself fortunate that in both my professions – as an economist and as a film-maker – I had the opportunity of coming in close contact with these two great personalities. I have learned a lot from being with them, observing them. Soumitra-kaku often spoke to me of his veneration for the work done by Amartya-da. Once, in an interview he was referred to as 'greatest living Bengali'. An exasperated Soumitra-kaku protested, "I feel very embarrassed to be described thus when another Bengali like Amartya Sen is still around."

I had invited Soumitra-kaku for the screening at Nandan. "The organizers want you to be the chief guest," I told him on the phone.

He replied, "Suman, will I be required to speak on the occasion? It will be impossible for me to say anything in his presence."

I said, smiling to myself, "We will see about that. You just come."

At the same time, whenever I spoke to Amartya-da about Soumitra-kaku, I sensed that besides his respect for Kaku as a thespian, he also nurtured a brotherly feeling for Kaku. When the two met at the function, Soumitra-kaku was like an obedient student in front of

Amartya-da. Amartya-da also looked very pleased at meeting him. His first question was, "How is Sambit?"

Sambit was Soumitra-kaku's elder brother. I discovered that he and Amartya-da had studied together in Presidency College. Together they also used to edit a journal. Thus, Soumitra-kaku was like a younger brother to Amartya-da. Only now did I realize the reason for the brotherly feeling I mentioned earlier.

But this personal link alone is not enough to understand the entire gamut of their relationship. There was something special about their bonding. I have often wondered at the unusual similarities between these two Bengalis. First, both of them were steeped in what I can only call 'Rabindra-consciousness'. It won't be an exaggeration to say that they were the true, worthy inheritors of Rabindranath Tagore's legacy. Thoroughly influenced by Tagore's philosophy, thoughts and world-view. Second, both of them have passed through the same history. I am aware of at least two such incidents from the history of Bengal that influenced them enormously: the great famine of 1943 and the Bengal riots of 1946.

Amartya-da specifically referred to the second in his Nobel lecture: "As a child, I was witness to a few scenes of that merciless cruelty. One afternoon in Dhaka a man entered our house through the main gate, screaming, bleeding profusely. It was heart-rending. That wounded man, Kader Mian, stabbed in the back, was a Muslim daily wager. He had come for some casual work at one of our neighbours' place to earn a few rupees. Some communal miscreants in our Hindu-dominated area had stabbed him ... the experience shattered me. It also made me aware of the dangers inherent in the divisive mentality engendered by politics arising out a narrow communal and individual identity." Soumitra-kaku had also time and again narrated stories of the 'Kolkata killings' of 1946. The incidents had troubled him deeply. The wound was so deep that in their later life it was their prime concern to raise their voice against communalism, to take a stand against the evils of communalism.

And about the Bengal famine, Amartya-da writes: "In the Bengal famine of 1943 around two to three million people died. I was then at Santiniketan. That memory still pounds my heart. Its utterly class-based character astonished me even then." Soumitra-kaku told me how the cry of '*Maa, ektu fyan dibi, fyan*' – the pitiable entreaty for a little rice gruel – tormented him all his life. Years later, Amartya-da wrote the book, *Poverty and Famines*, creating a sensation with its research on the prevention of famines.

At the same time, consider Satyajit Ray's film *Ashani Sanket*, which created a sensation with its stark depiction of the Bengal famine, and went on to win the Golden Bear at the Berlin Film Festival. What a nuanced performance by Soumitra Chatterjee it had. Working in two different fields, these two seem to be one in their ideologies and the way they look at the world. We find them epitomizing a culture – the conscience and intellectuality – of which Bengalis were at the vanguard.

It is for this reason that I feel it necessary to think of these two people at this moment. When people are playing fast and loose with icons of Bengali history, it is time to remember that perhaps these two are among the most important contemporary icons of Bengal. If there are still any Bengalis who can make a difference at the international level through their work, it is the duo of Amartya Sen and the recently deceased Soumitra Chatterjee. Let us not forget the message they have given us through their work.

# Interlude

## Ray Stories

Satyajit Ray and Soumitra Chatterjee formed one of cinema's most enduring and successful director-actor partnerships. Though their professional work together fascinated me, what I found as intriguing was their personal relationship. I often asked Kaku about this, in particular, if there had been any strain or tension in their interactions, ever. After all, it was a creative association that lasted over thirty years and fourteen films. Was it all smooth sailing?

Soumitra-kaku mentioned an incident during the making of Aranyer Din Ratri. For some reason, Kaku wasn't quite up to shooting one day - probably he was tired or feeling unwell. He told one of Ray's assistants that he would like to reschedule his sequences for the next day. What upset Kaku was not only that Ray did not acquiesce with his request, but instead of telling him so directly, instructed his assistant, within Kaku's earshot, to can the shots that day itself. Before turning to Soumitra-kaku to tell him that the shots had to be done that afternoon. Interestingly enough, on another occasion, Kaku was feeling ill but was unable to broach the matter with Ray given his experience at the time of Aranyer Din Ratri. But this time, almost sensing Kaku's condition, Ray suggested on his own that they postpone Kaku's shots to the next day. I found that rather interesting.

*Another incident Kaku recalled happened a few years later. He was by now a major mainstream star who commanded a good price and had a number of offers in hand. Working in a Ray film meant letting go of a few commercial ventures and there was a financial aspect to it. Ray's production manager had come to meet Kaku to discuss a project. Of course, Ray worked under severe budgetary constraints and Kaku was aware of that. However, he told the production manager that he wouldn't be able to lower his fees any further – he was already sacrificing a few films to take up Ray's project. The production manager communicated this to Ray. When Kaku met Ray over their next adda, he brought up the matter and mentioned how given his budget he wouldn't be able to afford more than what he had offered. Kaku told me, "I couldn't let him go on ... I felt so embarrassed about having brought up money with Manik-da. I just requested him not to worry, and that what he had offered was enough." I thought that the subtle manner in which the prickly issue was resolved said a lot about both men.*

*At the same time, I was always intrigued by the aura that Ray radiated. I had never met Ray, but in my mind's eye, he came across as someone in complete control over himself, over his circumstances. I often wondered if there was any moment when Ray had felt vulnerable, emotionally distraught. More specifically, if Soumitra-kaku recalled ever seeing Ray cry. Kaku mentioned just the one time. This was when Ray's mother passed away. All of us know that his mother was instrumental in raising Ray against all odds and in the face of many hardships after his father passed away when Ray was barely three years old.*

*Soumitra-kaku had gone to meet him and that's the only time he saw Ray on the verge of tears. But he overcame that moment admirably and started talking about work, mentioning some script that he had sent Soumitra-kaku. Then, after a brief pause, he told Kaku, "Work is all there is – that's the only solace." Much like Kaku found comfort in his work during some of his most trying times.*

# 9

# The Many Faces of Soumitra Chatterjee

## My Favourite Ten

### Introduction

Whenever Soumitra Chatterjee's acting career is discussed, particularly outside Bengal, it focuses primarily on the work of Satyajit Ray. I observed this after reading the obituaries in many international and national media outlets after he passed away. There is no doubt that he was indeed introduced by Ray in his iconic *Apur Sansar* and subsequently essayed many memorable roles in Ray films like *Charulata, Devi* and *Ashani Sanket* to name a few, but to Bengali film lovers he is much more than that.

He was a mainstream star along with Uttam Kumar and part of many excellent films transcending genres made by a wide range of directors. Since a lot has been written about his association with Ray, I thought it would be interesting to focus on his work outside the Ray oeuvre. With that in mind I created this list for audiences interested in his work beyond Ray. This is purely a personal list which tries to cover the vast vista of his work. Starting from his early films which established himself as a popular star (*Saat Pakey Badha*), to his persona as a romantic hero (*Basanta Bilap, Barnali*), his seminal performances in so-called 'arthouse' films (*Atanka, Ekti Jiban, Dekha* and *Paromitar Ekdin*), to the game-changing commercial success which turned around the Bengali film industry recently (*Belaseshe*), to perhaps his best performance in recent times (*Mayurakshi*) and finally the groundbreaking short film by Sujoy Ghosh (*Ahalya*).

I doubt whether any contemporary actor has had such a variety to boast of – and all this apart from the great Ray films. A list is always an 'iffy' affair with hits and misses and I had to keep out many seminal films of Soumitra-kaku like *Akash Kusum, Wheel Chair, Jhinder Bondi, Sansar Seemantey* and *Kony*, to name a few. So it is best to treat this list as a starting point to explore the entire breadth of his work.

***Saat Pakey Badha*, 1963**
**Director: Ajoy Kar**

I think this is one of the best mainstream films to have come out of Bengali cinema. Suchitra Sen was already a phenomenon after her thundering success with Uttam Kumar in films like *Harano Sur* and *Saptapadi* (both directed by Ajoy Kar). *Saat Pakey Badha* garnered her the best actress award at the Moscow International Film Festival. The film narrates the story of a couple, Archana (Suchitra Sen) and Sukhendu (Soumitra Chatterjee), whose marriage comes apart thanks largely to the Archana's domineering mother played by Chhaya Debi. Archana's mother has dreams of her daughter being married to a rich husband and thereby maintaining her status in society. Alas, Archana falls in love with and marries Sukhendu, a college teacher with a meagre salary, against her mother's wishes. All of this is pretty standard trope in popular cinema, but what singles out this film is the realistic portrayal of a marriage slowly crumbling against the inherent wishes of the couple.

Soumitra Chatterjee plays the husband who keeps his dignity intact amidst all the barrage of insults from his mother-in-law. It is easy to succumb into portraying a 'henpecked husband' in such scenarios as we have seen in numerous other films but he does not cross the line ever. I must confess that I found the characterization of the mother-in-law a bit too caricaturish in a film that etches all the other characters so well. Nonetheless, both Suchitra Sen and Soumitra Chatterjee are spot-on. As happens in any marriage, the initial love wears out over time, in this case because of the man's mother-in-law, and disagreements surface. At several moments they engage in caustic exchanges which are purely spur-of-the moment, which they probably regret later. The chemistry between them is perfect even in such scenes, aided by brilliant dialogues.

There is one scene involving Soumitra-kaku which is particularly striking. Amidst such tension in their relationship, Sukhendu tries to be gracious and make up with Archana. The way Soumitra-kaku changes his body language from a stern principled college teacher to a coy pampering husband is remarkable. Of course all the effort is wasted when his wife does not respond adequately, as often happens in relationships where right timing is of the essence.

There is also a fantastic scene towards the end of the movie when the results of the university exams are declared and Archana is the only one who receives a first class. This is after their divorce. Archana has decided to pursue a career in academics. Another old teacher comes and tells Sukhendu how proud he is, not because Archana has got a first class, but because Sukhendu is her husband. Clearly the teacher does not know their current marital status. In the entire scene the camera just focuses on Soumitra-kaku's face, so many emotions flowing seamlessly in his reactions. I liked the fact that he has absolutely no dialogue in the scene. He is obviously elated by the results, he still loves Archana, and he has to hide the fact that they are not together anymore from the other teacher. All of this in a thirty-second scene where he does not utter a single word.

I select this role as one of his major contributions more so because he is not the protagonist of the film. The film is told from Archana's point of view with voiceovers rendering her inner thoughts at times. I doubt whether Uttam Kumar would have done this role since by that time he was at the peak of his stardom with many superhits to his credit. In contrast, Soumitra Chatterjee was still relatively new in the Bengali commercial film scenario. Of course he had a dream entry in Bengali cinema, rather world cinema, with his films with Satyajit Ray. But in 1963 he had hardly had any solo hits to be considered a star. His greatness in *Saat Pakey Badha* is that without his 'jugalbandi', Suchitra Sen's performance would have fallen flat. Oftentimes that is more important and difficult to do than playing the protagonist. Soumitra Chatterjee nails it in this film.

### ***Barnali*, 1963**
### **Director: Ajoy Kar**

A young man invites a wrong family to the wedding of his uncle's daughter. After the error is discovered, the uncle – an insecure social climber who believes that the presence of a mere schoolteacher at his daughter's wedding will diminish his prestige – asks his nephew to uninvite the family and make sure that they don't turn up for the wedding. The young man is a doctor named Ashesh (played by Soumitra Chatterjee) and the loving family of the schoolteacher comprises a couple with two daughters, the elder being Aloka (Sharmila Tagore).

Ashesh finds out that Aloka is engaged to his friend Saileshwar (N. Viswanthan), a rather dubious character. What makes it even more interesting is that Aloka's fiancé (at least that's what she thinks) is the groom of Ashesh's uncle's daughter for which he had mistakenly invited Aloka's family. Aloka is clueless about this. This is the basic premise of the film (from a story by the brilliant writer Subodh Ghosh), a masterpiece in plotting. With this simple yet intriguing plot it manages to grab the interest of the viewer but soon the story structure evolves into an evening of charming delight with the two protagonists, the legendary pair of Soumitra Chatterjee and Sharmila Tagore, enacting their roles with an almost divine grace. No wonder legendary critic Pauline Kael described Soumitra Chatterjee and Sharmila Tagore as 'modern figures with overtones of ancient deities'. This latter part of the film at times reminds me of the brilliant films of Richard Linklater, *Before Sunrise* and *After Sunset.*

Circumstances play out in a manner that Aloka's family is invited to the wedding after all and just in the nick of time, when the bridegroom arrives, Ashesh manages to take Aloka away from the wedding venue so as to save her the humiliation of having to see her fiancé as the groom. Good drama arises out of several things in such a context, but the two most important elements are the asymmetry of information among the protagonists and the fact that they cannot express their true emotions given the circumstances. In this case, Ashesh cannot express his feelings for Aloka since it would seem selfish at such a juncture. But the director's ingenuity lies in how he uses these aspects so optimally throughout the film, aided by small gestures and crisp dialogues that keep the audience rooting for the pair to come together. All of this with a great aesthetic control.

The relationship between Aloka and Ashesh evolves organically. Aloka realizes that Ashesh has feelings for her which she clearly dampens by telling him that she is engaged. Then Ashesh finds out about her dubious fiancé and has to protect her from being hurt. There is a basic humane goodness combined with developing feelings for her which is brought out so well by Soumitra-kaku. The psychology of both characters is very deftly handled. Initially, Aloka suspects Ashesh's intentions in bringing her to his house but slowly she realizes the nobility of Ashesh. She is apologetic while Ashesh then becomes a bit upset on her. This constant ebb and flow of feelings is what creates the mood of the film.

There is an almost twenty-minute section with the two of them galivanting across the streets of Kolkata and even taking a boat ride on the Ganga which culminates in a beautiful song (*'Jakhon Bhanglo Milano Mela'*) that aptly captures their mood. They never express their feelings for each other directly but then that is the beauty. The song is picturized primarily as close shots of both of them, and through subtle nuances of their eyes they express their love. Pure brilliance.

### ***Basanta Bilap*, 1973**
### **Director: Dinen Gupta**

Audiences associate Soumitra-kaku with serious films with directors of the calibre of Satyajit Ray, Mrinal Sen, Tapan Sinha, Goutam Ghose, among others, though he was equally adept and hugely popular for his Bengali comedies too. As a film-maker I believe that the greatest test of an actor is how well he can perform comedy. Take any of the great Indian actors and one will find how they have excelled in comic roles. Naseeruddin Shah (*Jaane Bhi Do Yaaro*), Amitabh Bachchan (*Amar Akbar Anthony*), Kamal Haasan (*Michael Madana Kama Rajan*), Uttam Kumar (*Ogo Bodhu Shundori*), Irrfan Khan (*Hindi Medium*), to name a few. To perform in comedies, three things are crucial as an actor: timing, improvisation and fluidity. Those in the acting profession will appreciate how difficult it is to master these elements.

Among his many performances in comic roles, I personally think that Soumitra-kaku's best is in this slapstick comedy from 1973, a huge hit of its time. A slapstick comedy is often more difficult to pull-off for any director since it can easily morph into being loud and over the top. In *Basanta Bilap*, the director, Dinen Gupta, manages traversing the thin line with elan.

Though I mention Soumitra-kaku, in *Basanta Bilap* there was a bunch of other super talented actors with him who gelled so marvellously that the ultimate outcome was multiplied beyond individual brilliance. The performances of Robi Ghosh, Chinmoy Ray and Anup Kumar are etched in the memory of Bengali cine lovers. Who can forget those scenes when Chinmoy Ray tells his lover during courtship, "*Bolo ami Uttam Kumar*", or when Anup Kumar recites Jibanananda Das's famous poem 'Bonolota Sen' to his lover, brilliantly played by Sumitra Chatterjee, in a most bizarre rendition of the epic poem. And then there is the wonderful scene when Shyam (Soumitra-kaku) goes to the hostel camouflaged as an old man, where his true self is soon unearthed by the very smart girls in the iconic song '*Ami Miss Kolkata…*'. It is slapstick comedy at its best.

The story is pretty simple. A group of young men (with Soumitra-kaku leading the gang) are at loggerheads with a group of female residents of a hostel (their team headed by Aparna Sen). After many hilarious antagonistic exchanges, each of them gradually falls in love, except Shyam and Radha (Aparna Sen). That happens at the wonderful climax at the railway station when Shyam sacrifices going to Delhi for his love for Radha. On a personal note, I miss the 'Samapta' (The End) sign at the very end of the film which I feel is particularly soothing for a comedy with a happy ending as in this one. Those happened in films of yesteryears – I wonder when that tradition disappeared.

Unfortunately, such films did not travel beyond Bengal and hence they did not get the attention they truly deserve. Somehow Hindi remakes of these films also never materialized and so people outside Bengal have no clue how Soumitra-kaku made a fundamental contribution in the world of slapstick comedies too.

***Atanka*, 1986**
**Director: Tapan Sinha**

There is a famous quote of Rabindranath Tagore which says, "*Onnai je kore aar onnai je shohey, tobo ghrina jeno tarey trinoshama dohey*" (The one who commits a crime and the one who puts up with it should be equally condemned). Tapan Sinha's brilliant film revolves around this thought. The story is based on real-life incidents which stirred Sinha into making a film. Soumitra-kaku plays the role of a retired, upright and honest schoolteacher who happens to witness a murder being committed. Not only is he shocked by the heinous crime but what also deeply affects him is that the murderer is his one-time student –

and a bright one at that. He is threatened by the gang, "*Mastermoshai, apni kintu kichhui dekhenni*" (Sir, you have not seen anything) – which becomes a larger comment on the many ills we 'observe' in society and yet remain silent. Subsequently he faces an ethical dilemma – whether to report the crime to the police as a moral citizen or to protect his family (he lives with his son and daughter) in the face of constant threats by the miscreants.

It is at such a juncture that one of his young students recites those lines from Tagore which jolts Mastermoshai's conscience. I first watched this film when I was a school-going kid and somehow that threatening line – "*Mastermoshai, apni kintu kichhui dekhenni*" – stuck in my youthful mind. Recently, on a second viewing years later, I realized how contemporary the film has remained, even thirty-five years after it was made, given what we are going through in our country at present.

Soumitra-kaku was a man whose moral and ethical commitment against injustices in the world has been unparalleled. He always raised his voice, whether regarding the Bengali film industry, or the atrocities of any political party or any societal evil. A few years back when forty-nine well-known citizens of India, which included Mani Ratnam, Adoor Gopalakrishnan, Ramchandra Guha, Aparna Sen, Anurag Kashyap, among others, wrote a letter to Prime Minister Narendra Modi against mob lynching all over India, Soumitra-kaku was also one of the signatories. Given the general atmosphere of fear prevailing in the country, that voice of dissent is so crucial. But the decision to come out and speak the truth is not always easy. The powers that be often come at you with such vengeance that it makes the act of 'speaking up' quite difficult as demonstrated by what happened to the likes of Shah Rukh Khan and Anurag Kashyap, to name a few. They were silenced by indirect threats and other vicious means. That makes the story of *Atanka* so topical. We as a society have become so immune to injustices that this film still makes a statement and an urge to make our voices heard.

Soumitra-kaku captures this dilemma – whether to speak up or stay silent – brilliantly in the film. His decision to speak out comes at a huge cost. His daughter becomes the victim of an acid attack. The fear that Soumitra-kaku's facial expressions convey stands for the fear each one of us experiences when we take on the powerful. His performance makes it a universal experience for all of us who are equally scared of what is happening around us. The entire spectrum he covers – his fear, his fight with his conscience, his ultimately speaking up and reporting the crime – is a masterclass in acting.

Tapan Sinha is probably the only other director apart from Ray who explored Soumitra-kaku's potential as actor as no one else. Starting from the 1960 film *Khudito Pashan* to such important films as *Jhinder Bondi* (with the iconic Uttam Kumar), *Antardhan, Wheel Chair* and *Atanka*, this director-actor duo will be right up there as far as important collaborations in Indian cinema history are considered. It is quite fitting then that the year Soumitra-kaku won the National Award for best actor, Tapan Sinha was bestowed with the Dadasaheb Phalke Award.

### ***Ekti Jiban*, 1987**
### **Director: Raja Mitra**

*Ekti Jiban* is based on the life of Haricharan Bandopadhyay who is credited with having compiled the first comprehensive Bengali dictionary. It is the story of a man's obsession to complete the humongous task almost single-handedly. Amidst extreme penury, in spite of many trials and tribulations, including the death of his daughter, son and wife, Haricharan

Bandopadhyay kept at his goal almost as if possessed. It is one of Soumitra-kaku's best performances, Ray films included. It is a dream for any actor to showcase almost forty years of a protagonist's life and who better than Soumitra Chatterjee to carry the film on his shoulders. Apparently, Satyajit Ray also wanted to make this film but did not go ahead since he did not think that this range of age could be portrayed convincingly.

Before I go on to describe Soumitra-kaku's performance in the film let me digress a bit and talk about the main inspiration of the film's protagonist, incidentally also Soumitra-kaku's, namely, Ishwarchandra Vidyasagar.

The film shows that in trying times Gurudas (the name attributed to Haricharan in the movie) took solace from a photo of Vidyasagar in his house. I remember that in Soumitra-kaku's study there were two photos of personalities he considered his inspirations – Raja Rammohan Roy and Vidyasagar. Of course, Tagore was all pervasive in his life. We had several discussions on the contribution of Vidyasagar to Bengali society and culture, apart from his contributions to the Bengali language. Soumitra-kaku was a student of Bengali at Scottish Church College. I have not seen anyone with such a strong foundation and passion for the Bengali language. His command was on display in many of his writings and the numerous speeches that he gave during his lifetime. But the interest was much more deep-rooted and academic. I mention this since I am sure it contributed immensely to his preparation for the role.

His performance in the film is extraordinary except for one glaring aspect which I shall come to in a bit. Throughout the film the character traits of Gurudas change as he ages, and Soumitra-kaku captures that with impeccable detailing. Whether it is his gait, his body language or the brilliant make-up (by Ananta Das, Ray's frequent collaborator), one can see a man aging on screen convincingly. More importantly the mental transformation of Gurudas, wherein an idea becomes an obsession, an obsession almost a mental instability, is brought out with utmost honesty. This transformation takes over his life but he is unmoved. Nothing, no one, is able to distract him from his goal. Not that he is heartless, but that his belief in his mission is too strong for worldly griefs. There is one particular scene which is an absolute gem. After his daughter passes away, he is back to work on his dictionary – probably that is his only solace from the deepest recess of sadness. As he starts writing, teardrops smudge the ink. What a brilliant way to capture the complexity of the moment.

One thing which dampens an otherwise brilliant performance is Soumitra-kaku's voice at the end of Gurudas's life. He must be almost eighty years old at the time, but there is hardly any perceptible difference in his voice compared to what we have seen earlier in the film when he is middle aged. This directorial oversight is quite disappointing, in an otherwise brilliant film. How did it escape Soumitra-kaku? I never got around to asking him about this.

**_Paromitar Ekdin_, 2000**
**Director: Aparna Sen**

*Paromitar Ekdin* is probably my favourite Aparna Sen film. Among many other things that the film can boast of, I believe the relationship between the protagonist, Sanaka, played by Sen herself, and Soumitra Chatterjee's character (Moni-da) is rather unique. The information that we get from the film is that he was her brother's friend from their village. Clearly, there is an indication of him being an old flame but the relationship is portrayed with such admirable dexterity that 'flame' seems an inappropriate word. The dignity with which Soumitra Chatterjee plays the role when he frequently comes to meet her is class personified. Given that Sanaka is married into a conservative North Kolkata family, Moni-da's visits are not 'looked' upon well. The fact that he comes into their house is considered as crossing the boundaries of accepted societal conventions. Soumitra Chatterjee imbibes that aspect with great finesse in the reticence of his body language, in his gait, his soft-spoken dialogue delivery, and his postures. He walks with a slight limp which establishes his physical vulnerability aptly.

Though he does not have major screen time, five or six scenes at most, he makes his mark. There are scenes he plays so subtly that they get etched in the viewer's mind. Let me try to elucidate a couple of them. There is a scene where Rituparna Sengupta's (who plays Sen's daughter-in-law) character, Paromita, brings 'payesh' (a sweet dish made with rice) for him. There is a wonderful tentativeness expressed by Chatterjee before he accepts the payesh. Just some hand gestures and a hesitant smile – that's it. He is probably feeling guilty that she has made the effort to come down and cater to her guest at this odd hour but also wants to have the 'payesh' as he clearly is fond of it.

There is another brilliant scene when Sanaka's husband passes away and the camera shows Sanaka embracing Moni-da in grief. The beauty of the film is that it is replete with such moments where the characters' emotional mindscape is nebulous. The fact that Sanaka's relationship with her husband was at best tenuous, how was she feeling at his passing? Was there a tiny bit of relief? Again, the fact that her relationship with Moni-da was borderline scandalous in her conservative household and that she was embracing him made the scene even more impactful. Soumitra-kaku and Aparna Sen enact the scene with so much emotional power but without any sentimentality. It ends with Chatterjee taking a step back and retreating. Before he leaves he recites a poem which succinctly conveys the mood and his feelings. What a beautiful scene.

Finally one must mention the same tentativeness Chatterjee exhibits when he interacts with Sanaka's daughter, Khuku, played by Sohini Sengupta. The fact that she is mentally challenged in the film provides an avenue for the director to say certain things to Moni-da through her. She even mentions a physical aspect pertaining to her mother – that her body is soft and whether he would like to feel it. Chatterjee just reacts. One should watch his reactions as Khuku keeps blurting out unmentionable truths. A master class of acting through reacting.

Thus, through his interactions with the three women characters, portrayed by Aparna Sen, Rituparna Sengupta and Sohini Sengupta, Chatterjee fleshes out his character traits and makes it one of the most memorable guest roles in Bengali cinema.

***Dekha*, 2000**
**Director: Goutam Ghose**

This was my first foray into the world of Bengali cinema as I was an observer on the film. Hence, it has a special significance in my journey of life. This is also where I met Soumitra Chatterjee for the first time. Here, Soumitra-kaku's character (Sashi Bhushan Sanyal) is that of a former leftist poet who is disenchanted by how the world has evolved. Importantly, he has lost his eyesight, which is a significant comment from the director. He lives in a dilapidated North Kolkata mansion which is on the verge of crumbling and is a prime target for promoters, hovering like vultures, who want to build a multistoreyed building in that space. Another significant comment from the director about a way of life, a generation, being gobbled up by a nouveau rich society.

Part of his huge mansion is rented to the daughter of his teacher, played wonderfully by Debashree Roy, and her ten-year-old son Suman. At one point, Sashi Bhushan comments that he sees the world through the eyes of Suman and that provides him sustenance in an ambience he barely recognizes anymore. Sashi Bhushan exhibits such qualities as compassion, love, principles, ethics and a certain idealism that is distinctly lacking in today's world. Soumitra-kaku brings out these qualities in his portrayal with brilliance. The fact that he is blind ties him up significantly as far as an actor's tool is concerned as he can't use his eyes throughout the film. Interestingly, though he is handicapped in that aspect in a conventional sense, by not using his eyes in a traditional way he makes his gaze elucidate disgust, frustration, compassion and love. That is the hallmark of a great actor.

Another interesting thing to note is that there is one more actor in the film who is blind. However, unlike Sashi Bhushan, who becomes blind in middle age, this man was born blind. Of course, the mannerisms and behaviour in the two cases would vary. As far as I know, the other person who plays the blind character was really blind and not a professional actor. That makes the comparison more potent and if one pays close attention one can notice the difference in Soumitra-kaku's portrayal of a blind person who is not born blind.

After rewatching the film I kept wondering about Soumitra-kaku preparations for the role. Did he physically practise walking in his house figuring out things? Did he do a lot of research by talking to blind people or discussing with ophthalmologists? What was the mental preparation for the role? What was the exact communication that took place between Goutam Ghose and him? I regret that we never discussed this in our numerous addas. But that is what interests me a lot – the preparation that goes into the portrayal of such a remarkable role.

One cannot end the discussion of his performance in *Dekha* without mentioning the National Awards. That year he got a 'special mention' for *Dekha* which he refused. I would say rightfully so since the best actor award went to Anil Kapoor for the most undeserving *Pukar*. Soumitra-kaku officially commented later about the lobbyism which was an integral part of the National Awards. He went on to say that a "National Award is not an honest appreciation of someone's skill". After he received the best actor award for my film *Podokkhep*, he said in an interview with Rediff (3 July 2008), "My performance in *Podokkhep* is one of my best but certainly not my best. I have done fourteen films with Manik-da (Ray). And if you let me be the judge, I put in my best efforts in Ray classics like *Devi* and *Charulata*. Even my roles in non-Ray films like *Sansar Seemantey* and *Ekti Jiban* deserved to be recognized but weren't." I agree with his assessment.

### ***Belaseshe*, 2015**
### **Director: Shiboproshad Mukherjee and Nandita Roy**

Soumitra-kaku once told me a story about Satyajit Ray. Ray had been to a screening of a mainstream film of Soumitra-kaku's, one that Ray was unlikely to like. After the screening, when Soumitra-kaku asked him about his impression, Ray actually chided him. Apparently there was a scene where Soumitra-kaku was on screen but two other actors were having a dialogue exchange. Ray pointed out to him that he should have been alert since it was clear that he was not concentrating on the scene. When Soumitra-kaku told him that this was hardly a movie perceptive audiences would watch, Ray told him in a stern voice, "Listen, Soumitra, you are a professional actor. Whether it is my film or someone else's whom you do not regard much, it is your responsibility as an actor to deliver 100 per cent. You cannot be dishonest to your craft." Soumitra-kaku was taken aback as he did not expect this reaction from his mentor. Ever since he always remembered this advice, rather scolding, and he never repeated his mistake.

I mention this since *Belaseshe* is a movie Soumitra-kaku did not principally agree with. Not only in an aesthetic sense but he told me that it was morally and ethically wrong to pry upon your parents with a hidden camera – the basic theme the film addressed. But since the makers visualized it that way, he went along with it. The important thing to note is that Soumitra-kaku gave 100 per cent to the film. In fact, I doubt the film could be made without him. What is very important about this film is that it was a landmark hit. Few films in recent years have changed the landscape of Bengali cinema as this one did. At a time when potboilers were not working, and they are so crucial for the sustenance of an industry, this film showed the way for what a mainstream film could do. And Soumitra-kaku always mentioned that though he had some issues with the content, it was much better than the remakes of films from the south. It had an original 'Bangaliana' which appealed to the audience. Interestingly, the film also charmed a huge mass of non-Bengali cine-goers in Bengal.

I have to make a mention of Soumitra-kaku's acting style in this film. I found it quite astonishing that though the aesthetics of the film were a bit loud, Soumitra-kaku did not alter anything of his acting style fundamentally. He just captured the truth of the moment and believed in it wholeheartedly. This is an important lesson for actors. I have seen many who change their acting styles based on the type of film but fail miserably in the process. Forcing oneself to become melodramatic does not help in getting to the 'truth'.

For all of the above reasons I have included *Belaseshe* in this list. It also proved that an eighty-year-old actor could still rule the box office.

### *Ahalya*, 2015
### Director: Sujoy Ghosh

Fresh from his 2012 landmark hit *Kahaani*, Sujoy Ghosh embarked upon a different format of film-making which made history. The last I checked, his short film *Ahalya* had close to 20 million views, far higher than any other Indian short film on YouTube. It heralded the era of short films in India, but no other film could replicate the success of *Ahalya*. Based on an incident from the Ramayana, this fourteen-minute film stars Soumitra Chatterjee, Radhika Apte and Tota Roy Chowdhury. Before discussing the film and Soumitra-kaku's performance in *Ahalya*, let me digress and give some backstory of the very interesting relationship between Sujoy and Soumitra-kaku.

Sujoy is a close friend and I can vouch that I have hardly seen anyone which such solid knowledge of Bengali films, even non-significant ones. Apparently, when he was a student at Manchester many years ago, he somehow got access to many VHS cassettes of Bengali films and partly out of nostalgia and partly for nurturing the pure 'Bangali' in himself, he devoured all those movies. Ever since he has been a wild fan of Soumitra Chatterjee. Once when Soumitra-kaku, Sujoy and myself were having dinner together, I was very amused that even Soumitra-kaku did not remember the films Sujoy was mentioning. Over that dinner, Sujoy and I also discovered that when we received a call from 'Soumitra-kaku' both of us stood up out of pure respect before taking the call, as if Soumitra-kaku could see us.

After *Kahaani* released, Sujoy made it a point that his guru sees the film. He made special arrangements for Kaku in a theatre in Kolkata. After seeing the film Kaku was immensely impressed. He told me so many times about the brilliance of the film, its cinematography, the editing, the performances and its general smartness. According to him no one had showed Kolkata like *Kahaani* had done. Sujoy was clearly overjoyed. But his wish – to work with Soumitra Chatterjee – was still unfulfilled. Hence, he embarked on his first Bengali-language movie, *Ahalya*, with his guru in the lead role.

Given the nationwide mega success of a short film, that too in Bangla, *Ahalya* will go down in the annals of the history of Indian cinema. To imagine that a person who started his career with *Apur Sansar* in 1959 was now a crucial part of a revolution in short films as late as 2015 is history in itself. *Ahalya* is such a witty film that plays with the audiences mind in a unique fashion and one can see how Soumitra-kaku's performance is so instrumental in that. The way he delivers the dialogues keeps one guessing as to his real motive. Is he serious or is he just playing a game with the police officer? That's the charm of the movie till the end and how well Soumitra-kaku teases the audience.

## *Mayurakshi*, 2017
## Director: Atanu Ghosh

A middle-aged man, Aryanil (Prosenjit Chatterjee), with a chronic history of failed marriages, comes to Kolkata from Chicago to visit his father, a renowned historian named Sushovan (Soumitra Chatterjee), who is now eighty-three years old, and who has just begun to show signs of geriatric dementia and cognitive dysfunction. Sushovan's housekeeper Mallika (Sudipta Chakraborty) informs Aryanil that he has been asking for someone named Mayurakshi lately, although no one knows who the said person could be. This is the basic premise of the brilliant film by Atanu Ghosh, who is credited with some memorable performances of Soumitra Chatterjee in recent times in his films and telefilms.

Let me give a description of a scene from the film. Aryanil and Sushovan are chatting in a cafe. There is a shot of a teenage couple having a conversation outside the cafe. His father says that there are certain moments in life when one needs background music. Sushovan starts enacting the strokes of a violin accompanied by a scintillating music track. After Sushovan stops his 'performance', he stoops down and keeps something on the floor which befuddles Aryanil since there is no object in his hand. Reacting to Aryanil's curious expression, his father says, "*Violin ta namiye rakhlam.*" (I kept the violin down.) The scene ends with a shot of a brilliant expression of Aryanil, which has so many emotions captured in one. This scene will be remembered for years as one of the best cinematic moments one has seen. It proves that one can create such cinematic brilliance without special effects, graphics or breathtaking shot-taking. One needs just acute cinema aesthetics.

At eighty-three, Soumitra Chatterjee gave one of the best performances of his career. It reminded me of Julianne Moore's portrayal of an early onset of Alzheimer's in the film

*Still Alice*. In fact, Soumitra-kaku used to mention Moore's performance quite often in our addas. One feels the helplessness of the character as if one is experiencing it. How he goes into varied emotions throughout the film – through the use of body language, his eyes, and variations of his dialogue delivery – has to be seen to be believed. To convey the emotions that such a patient of dementia experiences, delving into his past and then immediately coming back to the present, is extremely challenging. His portrayal makes the audience empathize with the character which is indeed the crux of the film.

This is not your run-of-the-mill film. It does not have a well-defined plot, it does not have action, it does not have melodrama, the ending is not well-defined in a conventional sense but what it has is a pure cinematic experience. Many of the standard fare churned out in Bengali films these days aims towards the lowest common denominator. As a result the audience is losing the patience and ability to explore new modes of experiencing cinema.

I have heard from Soumitra-kaku that Satyajit Ray used to say that film-makers should take one step forward and the audience also should take one step forward. That is how our cinematic culture will be enriched. Atanu Ghosh took a big step towards that through *Mayurakshi*, on the able shoulders of a certain Soumitra Chatterjee. Watching Anthony Hopkins play an Alzheimer-stricken character in *The Father* recently, I could not help but think how overjoyed Soumitra-kaku would have been had he lived to watch the film. Hopkins was an actor he admired immensely and I am sure we would have a lot to discuss about *The Father* and Hopkins's performance in it.